"This is an absorbing gli_____ _____ alpinism. Shatayev's poetic pen demonstrates that once out of base camp the Russian mountaineer, like comrades anywhere on earth, is moved by the need for high, wild terrain — not manmade rules and kudos."
—John Hessburg, Associate Editor, SUMMIT Magazine,
Staff Writer, *Seattle Post-Intelligencer*

"In *Degrees of Difficulty*, Shatayev provides Western readers with a glimpse of what it is like to become a climber in a regulated society. Climbers of any nationality can find perches in his intellectual and erudite discussions of why we climb. Shatayev grapples with [the] existential questions [of life] in the face of death in the mountains."
—Sally Moser, Associate Editor
ROCK & ICE Magazine

"I was fascinated by Vladimir Shatayev's book, the testimony of a top Russian climber. It recalled strongly for me our own British group's visit to the Caucasus in 1958 when we were able to contrast our own somewhat haphazard, freewheeling approach to the mountains with the disciplined and graduated Russian system leading up to the accolade of a Master of Sport. We also climbed Pik Kavkaz with his mentor Misha Hergiani, leaving on the summit a can with our names on a note, burned around the edges, which Shatayev recalls finding some years later! Mountaineers may be moved by different motives and aspirations, but it is always a delight to share in each other's experiences."
—George Band, President
The Alpine Club (London)

"This is a remarkable book, intelligent, informed and gripping. For the first time it explains how Soviet people become climbers from the inside, examining the high moral standards incorporated into best practice there. Yet ultimately it is a highly human story, woven around one of the greatest climbing tragedies of all time. For those of us who were there, it rehearses again hours almost too terrible to think on. Yet, like all tragedy in the serious sense, it leaves a residue of renewal and hope. At a broader level it is also highly informative about climbing in some of the world's most exciting ranges."
—Paul Nunn, Editor
MOUNTAIN Magazine

DEGREES OF DIFFICULTY

Vladimir Shatayev

translated from the Russian by
DEBORAH PIRANIAN

The Mountaineers
Seattle

The Mountaineers: Organized 1906
" ... to explore, study, preserve and enjoy
the natural beauty of the Northwest."

© 1987 by the Mountaineers
All rights reserved

Published by The Mountaineers, 306 2nd Avenue West
Seattle, Washington 98119

Published simultaneously in Canada by
Douglas & McIntyre Ltd.
1615 Venables St., Vancouver, B.C. V5L 2H1

Originally published in 1977 in the USSR
Literary adaptation in Russian by Ilya M. Yakubzon

Manufactured in the United States of America

Cover photo: Author Vladimir Shatayev in action
Title photo: Shatayev on the summit of Mt. Crosson, Alaska

Library of Congress Cataloging in Publication Data

Shatayev, Vladimir.
  Degrees of difficulty.

  Translation of: Kategoriia trudnosti.
  Published simultaneously in Canada by Douglas &
McIntyre.
  1.Shatayev, Vladimir. 2. Mountaineers—
Soviet Union—Biography. 3. Mountaineering—Soviet Union.
4. Mountaineering. I. Title.
GV199.92.S52A3   1987   796.5'22   87-14885
ISBN 0-89886-013-X (pbk.)

0 9 8 7
5 4 3 2 1

*Dedicated to the memory of my wife,
Master of Sports Elvira Shatayeva.*

"What do you find in the mountains?"
"The philosophers' stone."
—From a conversation between a
hiker and a climber

Contents

Publisher's Note		viii
Translator's Note		x
Foreword		xi

1.	Over My Head (1968)	1
2.	Oleg Abalakov's "Threshold" (1968)	24
3.	The Mountain Sickness: "Ratingomania" (1957–1958)	34
4.	The Brocken-spectra Phenomenon (1959)	53
5.	The Route to a Bittersweet Dream (1960)	66
6.	Strange Mountains (1957–1963)	80
7.	Degrees of Difficulty (1963–1964)	103
8.	The Winter Route (1965)	119
9.	The Moral Aspect of the Theory of Probability (1971)	130
10.	In Pursuit of the "Snow Leopard" (1971)	142
11.	Thoughts about the Living (1971)	152
12.	The Pamirs (1974)	161
13.	Catastrophe (1974)	179

PUBLISHER'S NOTE

Degrees of Difficulty is the first Soviet book on mountain climbing to be translated into English and published in the United States. The author, Vladimir Shatayev, is one of the Soviet Union's most prominent climbers. He recounts his climbing career from an awakening interest in the sport during childhood vacations in the Caucasus Mountains through his triumphs on such difficult summits as Ushba and the Peak of Communism. In the process, the book provides an insider's view of mountaineering in the Soviet Union—of the climbing bureaucracy, the Soviet rating system, and the country's most prominent mountaineers. Perhaps even more important, the book demonstrates that whatever institutional and political differences may separate climbers East and West, those differences pale beside their common fears and aspirations.

Climbing in the Soviet Union occurs through local clubs under the auspices of the Soviet Federation of Mountaineering. Though not directly supported by the government, the federation's activities are subsidized by labor unions from membership dues. Since there are no professional climbers in the Western sense, climbing is largely restricted to annual vacations. Climbers are ranked according to skill, and progression through the ranks occurs under the close supervision of coaches. Upon joining a climbing club, the novice receives a badge and is thus called a badge holder. After that, climbers are rated according to demonstrated ability. The lowest rating is the third rank, followed by second, then first. Each climber must demonstrate a certain level of ability before he or she is permitted by coaches to progress to climbs of the next degree of difficulty. The most accomplished Soviet climbers earn the title Master of Sport and are generally conceded to be comparable in skill to the better climbers in the West. Vladimir Shatayev is a member of this elite group.

Degrees of Difficulty is more than autobiography; it is one climber's attempt to come to terms with a sport that at any moment can, and too often does, claim the lives of companions, friends, and loved ones. Shatayev's personal loss was enormous. During the Soviet Union's 1974 International Camp in the High Pamirs of central Asia, his wife Elvira Shatayeva and seven other members of the Soviet women's team died in a freak snowstorm while attempting to scale 23,406-foot Peak Lenin.* The heart of the book is Shatayev's extraordinarily moving account of that tragedy; its soul is his attempt not merely to make sense of the loss but to survive it as a climber.

Degrees of Difficulty was published in the USSR in 1977. The Mountaineers would like to thank Leah Siegel for her assistance in obtaining the American rights to publish this book, Alex Bertulis for his encouragement and support in bringing the project to fruition, and Deborah Piranian for her skilled translation.

---

*A version of that event was told in Robert Craig's *Storm and Sorrow*, published by The Mountaineers in 1977.

TRANSLATOR'S NOTE

Every translator is faced with the problem of how close to stick to the original language and text and how much to adapt the text for readers who are not familiar with either that language or the culture associated with it. Because my approach was to translate into the most natural English possible, the result is not a word-for-word translation. However, I tried to retain the author's style, which is complex in its mixture of figurative and colloquial elements. I chose to omit certain references that were insignificant to the book as a whole. I used a simple, consistent system of transliteration so that names would be easier to read and remember. Most of the place names were transliterated except those with standard English versions, such as Moscow.

There is another point the reader might keep in mind. In Russian, wives' surnames often differ from those of their husbands by the addition of *a*. Thus the author's name is Shatayev and his wife's, Shatayeva.

I would like to express my gratitude to Solomon Ioffe, who was so patient in offering help as a native speaker of Russian. Without his vast knowledge of both the Russian language and Soviet culture this translation would not have been possible.

Foreword

It has been said that mountain climbing sometimes brings people together when governments cannot. The sport first brought American and Soviet climbers together in 1974, when the American Alpine Club received an invitation to send a delegation of U.S. climbers to the International Climbing Camp in the Pamirs Range, which hugs the Chinese and Afghan borders. No American and few Europeans had climbed in the Pamirs since the Russian Revolution, so the occasion was seen as an unprecedented opportunity to establish ongoing mountaineering relations between the two nations.

Nineteen carefully selected U.S. climbers journeyed to the remote central Asian plateau where the Hundu Kush, Tien Shan, and Himalayan ranges converge. The tent compound that sprang up in that alpine meadow at 11,700 feet was like a United Nations of mountaineering, as 160 of the world's climbers from 12 nations gathered. Vladimir Shatayev of the Soviet delegation was prominent among those world-class climbers.

That summer of climbing was not particularly distinguished in mountaineering history, but it launched an exchange of U.S. and Soviet climbers that continues today. Numerous U.S. teams have climbed in the Soviet Union in the past few years and several Soviet delegations have visited the U.S., where they've climbed our highest and hardest peaks. I, along with other American climbers, have been privileged to host Soviet alpinists in my home and I believe the cultural sharing has been eye-opening for both Americans and Soviets.

Just as I've enjoyed meeting these visiting climbers, I've enjoyed getting to know the "inner Shatayev" through the pages of this book. Its publication is another landmark in the development of U.S.-Soviet climbing relations because for the first time, American readers can see the world of Soviet mountaineering through the eyes of a Soviet climber.

> Pete Schoening
> Leader, 1974 American Pamirs/USSR Expedition

1. Over My Head
(1968)

I rested awhile longer with my elbow against the compact firn, which had been swept clean by the wind. Suddenly I became angry at my own hands. They were senselessly and stubbornly resisting against my will, which had faded along with my strength and lay frozen with my spirit. I divorced myself from my hands and lowered myself onto my stomach, burying myself in the rough, compressed snow, which was similar to unrefined sugar.

Kavunenko and Piskulov were looking at the back of my head. It was good that they couldn't see my face; I wouldn't have wanted them to read on it everything that I was thinking about them, about myself, and about the stupid passion that had led us here...

They are ridiculous with their idiotic faith in this game. It's time to sober up, even here at seven thousand meters elevation. With age, one ought to gain something besides weight; in them, only naïveté grows. Nothing cools their ardor, not even this strange, dismal world of glaciers and rock, unfit for life, terrible and cold to the eye, where every molecule of oxygen is important. They want me to drag myself on all fours with them up another half kilometer... for a game that—it's clear to me now—is not worth the effort.

I grin because they think, He will lie awhile, rest, and get up, as always; but this time I won't get up. I have hypoxia, mountain sickness, and by all rights, and with a clear conscience, I don't have to get up. There, on the ground, they give people in my condition an oxygen mask . . .

It was 1968. The three of us were on the Peak of Communism, the highest summit in our land, for the first time. Until then I had always taken myself in hand and gotten up because I considered it important, not only for the ascent, but because, for each of us, the success of the climbing season depended on it. Now I understood the uselessness of such passions. They offered no more to my companions than they did to me. I thought, I will lie here and not stir; the rules of mountaineering oblige them to take me down.

I rolled over on my back and looked directly at the zenith of the strange, unearthly evening sky. It was not a sky. It did not have depth or transparency. It was a motionless, threatening ceiling, thickly painted ultramarine by a hack. Such a sky did not exist on earth. It seemed as if throwing a stone into it would make a hole.

In this vast, hardened world, sparkling with snow and ice and oppressive in scale, we were only three small, barely visible dots. One had only to be here in order to realize one's infinite smallness. And yet, like smudges, we stained the blinding whiteness.

I thought how dissimilar the Pamirs were to the Caucasus, which is cozy, domestic, and intimate, like the outlying streets of an old European city. Here in the Pamirs everything was huge and primordial; everything breathed with the freshness of creation. It seemed as though the Biblical "And there was light!" had just been spoken.

You lose a sense of distance there. You can't tell what is far away and what is close. There isn't any visual scale. Those distant spurs on the right may prove to be an hour's walk, while this nearby peak on the left may be days away. Only when you've dragged yourself there, over thousands and thousands of meters, when you don't understand whether the noise you hear is your gear banging or your bones, when your eyes drop into their sockets and you can't tell right from left—then the beauty fades, and the riddles and paradoxes are no longer intriguing. Those who go there know only two directions: downslope, back where they began, where human warmth and life still exist, and ahead, where neither abides.

I felt lucky. My thoughts were directed only in one direction—down to base camp where Yura Vizbor sings his songs and Doctor Hilkin tells anecdotes, where Oleg Abalakov remained, and where they had taken Sasha Voronov down from an elevation of 6,000 meters.

They had looked at us with open envy when we set off on this route with rucksacks and ice axes. Vizbor had gotten angry at the doctor for not letting him go higher than Peak Kosmonavtov. And Oleg—he, it seems, didn't come out of the tent at all. I understood his mood well: a second season of failure. The "Peak of Communism does not accept him," they were saying in camp. The first time Oleg was evacuated from 7,200 meters; he had become sick with less than 245 meters to go to the summit. This time he had managed only to reach the notch on the southwest ridge, along which we had first wanted to approach the summit. As they were returning to camp, he had jumped across an unpretentious crevasse and sprained his ankle. That was Oleg! Usually he looked like a virtuoso acrobat, even in comparison with other master rock climbers.

Four of us had later set off on the same route. Ours was not a first ascent; we were on Evgeny Tamm's path. And if one disregarded the Bivouac Glacier, where we had to jump across large crevasses and wander through a forest of seracs and fantastical ice trunks, then everything had gone rather smoothly at first.

By about five o'clock we had topped 6,000 meters, according to my altimeter. But it was still daylight, and we decided to make a dash for the plateau of Peak Pravda. There, at 6,200 meters, we dug a comfortable snow cave for the night. We dug eagerly, painstakingly, lovingly, and happily. We had enough strength then, and our route seemed the right way to the summit.

During dinner Voronov coughed. Kavunenko, gazing at his cup of tea, said, "Want me to guess what you have in your hand?"

Voronov was silent a moment, then replied sullenly, "What? I can't use my handkerchief?"*

"You're getting angry. You're not a novice in the mountains. You know how high-altitude problems end. Better speak now, before it's too late. Tomorrow we'll descend."

"I know I'm not a novice in the mountains, and *I* say I can walk!"

"Well, if you can, you can."

The next morning we set off under these circumstances. After several hours Kavunenko and I broke away from the second rope team and went way ahead. At 6,600 meters we decided to wait for Piskulov and Voronov. Piskulov arrived soon. But no Sasha Voronov. After some time passed, he appeared, barely dragging his feet. I asked him silently, with my eyes. He nodded.

We distributed Sasha's things among our own rucksacks, turned around, and started back down toward our cave at 6,200.

Diseases have free reign up high. Altitude is poetry to them. It's strange: At altitude the path of man is best measured by time, but the flow of sickness by space. Between the light irritation in the throat at the start and the asphyxia at the finish is an interval that is best measured with

---

*Kavunenko feared that Voronov was exhibiting the first signs of pulmonary edema, an acute form of altitude sickness. — The Editor.

a tape measure. The more meters above sea level, the more virulent the diseases. Every meter multiplies their strength. A cold at 8,000 meters can prove fatal. And while we stumble along, gaining centimeters, the diseases run with gigantic strides.

At the 6,200-meter bivouac we had a fortuitous meeting with a group descending from Peak Pravda. We asked the fellows to help Voronov down to base camp. The next morning we ourselves set out a little earlier on the way back up.

We left Sasha gloomy and dismal; I sympathized with him.

Funny — I *sympathized with* him! *Now, I understand that it was he who should have sympathized with us. I think that now, but then . . . then I had grieved for Sasha; I was glad it hadn't happened to me. "Then" was ten hours ago, when I was still annoyed with people who did not understand my passion for the summit. Now everything has reversed. What remained of the Shatayev of yesterday? Desires, feelings, manners, disposition — were they part of me only ten hours ago? Now, nothing remains besides a dry, emotionless memory of facts.*

"How are you?" Above me I heard the forced cheerfulness of Kavunenko's wheezy voice. "You must crawl out. Grab hold of a forelock and pull yourself out, like Munchhausen.* He was a real person; only his stories are dubious. You'll manage. This is not the first year you and I have been on the same team."

I was silent. The hypocrisy of this optimism angered me. This make-believe life, the romanticism, the false ideals and goals. Was it all just a game? Yes, but a serious one justified by only puzzling, speculative theories.

Kavunenko walked off. Together with Piskulov he cleared snow from the trough they had dug out for the night. They

---

* A German renowned for telling tall tales of his exploits. — The Editor.

worked without speaking; only their breathing was audible. They moved slowly and rested after every two or three shovelsful.

Piskulov approached me. "Can you go on?"

At first I was silent. Then I asked, "Can you?"

He did not answer. I raised myself on my elbows and, looking him in the eyes, asked, "Explain why I should. What is the point? So that they'll write 'Peak of Communism' on my card? If you can explain why, I'll get up. I'll clamber on all fours until my legs quit."

"What is there to explain? If I had asked you that this morning, you would have said, 'That's the philosophy of old age: to avoid risk, to just bide your time'."

"That was this morning, but now the spirit of that Shatayev doesn't exist!"

"Rubbish!" It was Kavunenko again. He approached and did not sit, but literally fell on his rear end. "Let him lie for another fifteen minutes. If he can't, we'll go down." Then to me, "Only bear in mind: It's not you but the lack of oxygen that is speaking. After all, you're a specialist in medicine. You probably used to tell the novices in camp, 'It is said that mountain sickness is accompanied by apathy—loss of appetite, not only for food, but for life as well'." He turned to Piskulov. "Let's go, Yura. Let him lie a little longer. He'll get up. I know him."

The philosophy of old age: to bide one's time and not truly live? No, that's the speculation of eccentrics. But they're right about one thing: Yesterday I really would have said something the same. I remember that much. So when was I sick, yesterday or today? The minute you start to speak seriously, eccentrics attribute all sorts of diseases to you.

Nothing hurts. I feel only weakness, like in a dream when you can't move, escape, chase, or defend others or yourself. I feel some sort of melancholic yet pleasant self-pity. And more . . . a strange sensation of the sluggish, lazy movement of my blood.

Over My Head (1968)

Even without Kavunenko, I knew it was mountain sickness. But I comprehended the connection between my disease and my reasoning only by means of a confused, even alien logic. I was without faith. I thought of the Russian proverb: "We have complete faith only in what we can feel."

Recovery lay back at base camp, for mountain sickness lessens with each meter downward, just as it grows with elevation. Only I wondered: Does it really make any difference?

Volodya and Yura stirred inside the cave, taking turns crawling in and out, dragging a parka loaded with snow. They did not approach me. Could fifteen minutes really last so long? Each time they appeared, I looked cautiously toward the exit. If they appear together, I thought, they will approach me; I must answer them—up or down. But I didn't want to go either direction, only to lie motionless and calm.

The person who sees happiness in peace is right. If only those two would. Why does it always happen that we can't be happy to the end? Some thing *always darkens it. Some* one *always darkens it. But the prospect of no one or no thing is frightening. In nature there is both honey and tar.*

Now I must say up or down, one of the two. The third way—to remain where I am—is desirable, like happiness, and is as close as my elbow. But the third is not allowed. Weakened and exhausted themselves, my companions won't let me have peace. Do they really believe that what is considered bad is good for me? They will say, "It's the philosophy of old age."

The philosophy of old age! The ravings of credulous infants. To remain alone and lie here. To lie here and nothing more. To think? Now I don't even want *to think. Only to lie here. The word* want *loses its meaning. I cease to understand it, as a satiated person ceases to understand the feeling of hunger. Desires desert me. When I don't even want to lie here, what then? What else can be left? What? "To bide one's time, but not to live."*

Suddenly I thought: My full, rounded consciousness will become flat, then linear, then slowly attenuate until all that is left is a dotted line. Then emptiness. I felt the emptiness in me, a spinning, nauseating, ever-churning emptiness, as if a sudden force were sucking out my insides, pulling them up toward my throat, filling my sunken thorax with thick, explosive fear.

Fear is disgusting when it oozes like a thin, meager trickle, when it eats away at the soul like splashes of acid, or when it penetrates the blood like a paralyzing poison. But a powerful, explosive fear, which does not appear always or to everyone, nourishes a man, gives him renewed strength, clarity of thought, the reflexes and precision of a mongoose; it makes him feel suddenly rejuvenated, endowing him with lifelong impressions of life fully and clearly. Whoever has experienced such fear knows that it is so. Fear *is* life! It is close to joy. At that moment I understood that. I understood too that fear had also brought me out of a state of indecisiveness and indifference and returned the will to struggle.

I shouted, probably too loud and hysterically. Kavunenko and Piskulov rushed to me, frightened. Yura was holding a saw with which he had evidently been cutting the firn.

I got up on my knees. How and when I managed to do it, I did not notice, but I felt that I could stand up straight on my feet. However, I did not get up. I realized that I should not do that; too big a strain at once and I could lose consciousness.

I rocked slightly. Piskulov, noticing this, said, "Lie down, lie down. We'll pack you up in a sleeping bag now and start down."

"Wait," Volodya interrupted him. "Well, have you decided?" He pointed at the summit. And not waiting for my answer, he slapped Piskulov on the shoulder. "I told you he'd get up."

"We have to descend, Volodya," said Piskulov.

Volodya looked at me happily, not paying attention to

Yura's words. Piskulov had not realized that this was not the first season that Kavunenko and I had climbed together.

I reached for the saw. Perplexed, Piskulov held it behind his back.

"Give me the saw," I said.

"Why?"

"He told you to give him the saw!" Kavunenko barked at him.

Movement, movement: That's what everyone says, both the theoreticians—the doctors—and the practitioners—the climbers. There's only one medicine, one salvation. Somehow to do something . . . sitting, lying down, on all fours.

Slowly and carefully I got up on my feet. The mountains suddenly moved from their places and leaned toward the horizon. It was as if I were looking through the window of a banking airplane and as if, balancing, the mountains went now up, now down. Kavunenko grabbed me from behind and said, "We have to go down."

"We don't have to."

I got up on my knees again and dragged myself on all fours to the small snow ledge about ten meters away. On the wall of the half-meter step, the dirty-gray, compacted layers were distinctly visible, as in the cross section of a tree.

The snow sawed easily. It's a pleasant thing if one's healthy; it's as soothing as it is invigorating: to cut out a snow cube of about thirty centimeters takes a minute, no more. I worked at it for an eternity.

The saw seemed heavy. It would not obey; it crumbled the edge into zigzags. I lay down to rest, and when I picked the saw up again it felt much lighter. And then I noticed that the sky above was warm and the mountains happy and entirely complacent. I thought, Everything happening to me here is good and right.

I dragged the first block of snow over to the cave entrance, having decided to build a small wall here in case of a strong wind. I walked back fully upright. From the cave to my "quarry" was no more than seven or eight meters. I had to rest halfway.

Snow sawdust was flying in all directions. It splashed into my face, striking pleasantly like tiny cool needles. I brought my face closer to my work.

After each rest my hand became firmer and more certain. But I tired easily, and the moment very quickly came when, exhausted, I lost the ability to guide my hand. It moved as if on its own, under the effect of a stubborn, dulled, unthinking desire. The saw would not cut then: it would crawl sluggishly, cutting away idly somewhere inside, not touching the snow with its teeth.

Played out, I thought decisively, Why the right hand? I can also do it with the left, although it's more difficult. It's good that it's harder. I need to do it with my left.

The saw went all over the place. The edge turned out to be broken and crooked. But was I really sawing? No, I was pumping my blood, dispersing it. It is difficult to chase one's own blood around one's veins. Strength departs. The hand grows numb; it almost doesn't move. It only seems to be moving. I just wanted it to really move.

I threw down the saw, sprawled on my back, and rested. Maybe it was not worth it? No, it was! After all, I had just pulled myself out of the worst. It was worth it. Another hour and a half of sensible work would be enough. Sensible! Without sorting things out, without reevaluating the possibilities, gradually accumulating time and shortening the rests, listening to myself as a piano tuner to an instrument... I took the saw and once again snow spray showered my face.

The wall turned out uneven. The fellows, sitting in the cave, watched me through the doorway and laughed—if one can call a limp distortion of an exhausted, cold, wind-hardened face a laugh.

I suddenly noticed my protection against the weather, and it would have made a cat laugh: the wind was blowing from the other side.

"The most valuable work is that of a monkey," Kavunenko said. "He's made a monkey into a man."

A true joke. The wall finally brought me to my senses. The attack of mountain sickness had lasted an hour and a half, but enough feelings and sensations and all sorts of details survived to last a year.

"A true joke," I said out loud. "Don't forget it when we're on our way to the summit."

"Is he actually planning to go to the summit?" laughed Kavunenko. "Keeps changing his mind," he added suddenly. "Prepare dinner, then."

At the word "dinner" Piskulov knit his brows and silently began to investigate his sleeping bag. Kavunenko stretched out his leg and placed it on the sleeping bag as if by accident. Yura tried to remove it, but Kavunenko resisted, feigning indifference by looking somewhere through the arch of the cave.

"One more," he said to me, nodding in Piskulov's direction. "It's catching." But turning sharply to Piskulov, he threw out angrily, "Stop playing the fool. First dinner, then sleep. He's barely recovered from mountain sickness and immediately you jump into the bag to die."

Yura immediately softened, and his breathing became openly labored and rapid. He wiped his sweaty face with the sleeve of his parka and sat motionless, dropping his hands to his knees. He too had been feeling bad up to now, but had struggled to hide it from Kavunenko. Now, when he knew that Kavunenko knew anyway, it did not make sense to hide it, and he let himself go.

I held out some vitamin-C tablets, but Piskulov didn't move.

"Well? Do we have to pry your mouth open with a knife?" Volodya said it sourly, without his usual firmness, as if strained to the breaking point.

Yura looked at him in surprise, placed a couple of tablets on his tongue, and began to move his jaws mechanically, carrying out the unpleasant but necessary business.

Kavunenko and I crawled out of the cave. The temperature had dropped rapidly. The vapor from our breath crystallized immediately and settled on our faces and collars, dusting them with rime.

I told Volodya that he had been too hard on Yura. The desire to hide the sickness had given Piskulov the strength to struggle with himself.

"Even if he could have lasted on that . . . "

Kavunenko took shelter by the snow parapet and was silent for a long time. It seemed to me that he was falling asleep. I touched him on the shoulder.

"Well, what! What! I'm thinking, thinking. This is all nonsense. You can't last on that. After half a hour you decide to be open. It's said that you can't hide it from the fellows. People are too easy on themselves, even when they're waging a war against themselves. You need roughness at that time. You need to drive yourself. And it's better if others drive you, get angry at you."

"One has to deal with oneself."

"'Has to!' Everything is 'has to' with you. Moralists! An hour ago there was nothing you had to do. You called mountaineering foolish. Maybe you were right."

I did not understand immediately. I waited for the last phrase to be turned into the usual caustic joke. But he looked to the side, afraid to look me in the eye. He was silent awhile and then lowered himself limply onto the snow and added, "I was joking. Don't worry."

I pretended that I believed him. But in my heart I was still suspicious of everything. "He's fighting not so much with Piskulov as with himself," I thought.

We still had one day of climbing to reach the summit—only half a kilometer in all. Only? That's five hundred meters up—a hundred and sixty-five stories, but not up ready-made stairs! Better not to think about it. Instead, think that behind us are more than six kilometers of vertical and a year of preparation. No, not a year, six years! Or more?

At that time I did not understand what was wrong with

Kavunenko: had mountain sickness gotten hold of him, or was it a reaction to extreme fatigue? I only saw him endlessly swallowing vitamins, and after dinner he reached several times for the water bottle with lemon drink. If it was mountain sickness, then he was dealing with it excellently.

A faded blue cloud, tight and bulging like the belly of a huge animal, rolled quickly toward us from the northwest, covering the orange edge of the evening sky. The wind blew in sharp gusts, becoming stronger with each one. Kavunenko suddenly stood up and said, "The wall still needs to be put in place. Get Yura over here. He and I will take care of it. Maybe we'll finish before the blizzard descends upon us."

Piskulov was asleep, sitting on the rucksack in the same position. His features had sharpened; his face was drawn and had taken on a strange bluish hue. And if it had not been for the heavy, wheezy breathing, one would have thought... He did not want to wake up; he gave me a crazed look and closed his eyes again. But I shook him. He was actually a good sport and gave me much less trouble than I had expected. He sat for a minute, collecting his strength, and, putting on his boots, crawled out of the cave.

For some reason, I thought, this fellow never becomes unreasonable under any circumstances. I recalled the mountaineering film I had seen in Moscow before leaving for the Pamirs. I had been struck by the hero's spiritual simplicity, which had been played up. It suggested that mountaineers were "simple folk," motivated only by simple courage. Afterwards I had often looked into my companions' faces, searching for something similar, but I saw only ordinary faces, like everyone else's.

Now I wonder where this stereotype, this identification of courage with the primitive, came from? Where did the opinion come from that courage runs thin where intellect exists? From boyhood perhaps, when arguments are settled with fists?

It is said that the greater a man's intellect, the stronger his fear. I think that's true. As the poet Heine has expressed fully yet succinctly: "Only a fool knows no fear." If fearlessness even exists, then it is only through lack of understanding and through an underestimation of danger. The expression "to scorn danger" has merit only for people who have not experienced it.

No, that is not courage. Rather, courage is the ability to keep going when fear, weakness, disbelief in oneself, and a refusal to fight stand as constant barriers.

Those who prepare themselves to assault a summit would not miss the opportunity to "jump across an abyss" once again. They have developed strength of character not just in passing, but intentionally and methodically, as a ballerina acquires eurythmics or a tightrope walker a sense of balance. This discipline is not for the lazy or narrow-minded. Such a person will not attempt it because his laziness will make him quick to label it as strange, ridiculous behavior. He will scornfully call the discipline "introversion" when actually it is "introspection." Such a person becomes acquainted with himself on the horizontal of the tram and recognizes only the vertical of the elevator. Not having received a substantial answer to the question "Why go into the mountains?" he will say "Smart people don't go into the mountains!"

According to statistics, about eighty percent of mountaineers have a higher education. Among them are Ph.D's, professors, writers, journalists, and laborers. The names of the academicians Aleksandrov, Vinogradov, Letavet, Khokhlov (the rector of Moscow State University), and the late Tamm are well known in mountaineering.... And if a higher education is still not grounds for calling an athlete an intellectual, then the fact that the overwhelming majority of climbers have a higher education gives one the right to call mountaineering the sport of the intelligentsia.

The stove was covered with hoarfrost and burning our fingers with cold. At high altitude, a climber always takes the stove out of its bag cautiously and anxiously. This "machinery of grandmothers," which has become the utmost symbol of the primitive and archaic, decides the fate of climbs and climbers. It is better to be deprived of food than to be without a stove, which thaws and warms us, inside and out. And at high elevation, boiling water is more valuable and "nutritious" than sturgeon caviar.

The stove, however, is a treacherously unreliable thing. Whether it heats up or not is pure chance. At times it does not burn because it is honestly broken, but at times it does not work because it does not work. Entire groups of high-altitude climbers, watching one of their members light the stove, await their sentence...

I filled it with gas and pressed the plunger on the pump. The plunger failed: it caught on something and would not move back into place. There was *our* sentence! Organisms chilled and weakened by hypoxia do not last. God forbid that by morning pneumonia, quinsy, or some other ailment that is dreadful at high altitude should appear in the group. One thing remained: to crawl into our sleeping bags and warm ourselves with our own heat, and in the morning, if the weather is good, to descend.

Like hell! I grabbed the stove and started to shake it. I tried the plunger—it wouldn't budge! Any minute a snowstorm would start. Any minute the fellows would crawl in with the hope of getting warm.

I lit a match on the off chance. A flame suddenly leaped up, flashed feverishly and noisily several times, and disappeared, flitting away in the arch of the cave. I shook the gas in the can and made a second attempt. The burner blazed up with a blue, energetic flame. The stove began to cough and roar, seemingly threatening to fly into pieces at any moment.

Bad weather seemed about to break loose. The wind whirled around, gathered strength, and became a blizzard. Everything around turned upside down.

Piskulov and Kavunenko tumbled in, choking, their faces covered with sleet. Kavunenko recovered his breath. "They say there's no heaven? But what's this?" he asked, touching the stove. "Well, he's got it stoked! Control the flame or we'll melt."

"You try to control it."

The thermometer in "heaven" showed minus eighteen, even under the influence of the stove. But the mercury column had already risen and was still rising rather quickly. The snow in the pot melted and became warm water. Yura Piskulov turned his mug in his hands, looking greedily at the water, but did not bring himself to dip in, fearing he would be "slapped on the hand." I took the pot from the stove and poured him about half a mug. He chugged it in one gulp and gave a sigh of relief.

Kavunenko watched Yura tipping his mug back as a tennis player watches a returned ball. Then, without counting on results, but more for humor, said, "And me? Sisyphus is being tortured by thirst."

"Be patient."

"Yes, the Greek gods were resourceful. They threw the work to Sisyphus. Well? Does the question remain open as to the meaning of our labor? Be quiet! Aren't you ashamed?" Kavunenko stretched out his long legs, rested his head on a rucksack, and, putting his hands under his head, started to speak, addressing himself and very pleased about something. "No, brothers. Sisyphus' labor is not so senseless. In his heart, he believed that at some time he would finish rolling his stone and receive forgiveness. Otherwise, no kind of force, not even divine, could have forced him to do it. He will finish rolling it. According to the theory of probability, the most improbable happens at some time. According to this theory, at a certain time the gods' incantations will not operate. Definitely! And Sisyphus will roll his stone to the very top. Definitely! Otherwise the theory of probability is not worth a penny. There is no such thing as meaningless labor. Someday it will become clear to everyone why we roll our 'stone' to the summit. Listen, Shatayev, give me a little water. Sisyphus is thirsty. Get this, it's not stated anywhere how much Sisyphus' stone weighed. On the other hand, everyone knows that there are no seven-thousanders in Greece. After all, I took thirty-three kilos, not by rolling, but strapped to my back, as far as eight thousand."

We were all suffering from an unquenchable thirst. In a state of oxygen starvation and an atmospheric pressure less than half of normal, when one's dog-tired and the heart is working its utmost, the body excretes an unusually large amount of moisture. On a high-altitude climb we each always lose five to seven kilograms in weight from dehydration.

The only hope is that the heart will endure. To overload the body with fat means to overload the heart. It figures that if you are going to drink water, you should drink it in the optimal form. Now it was necessary not only to quench our thirst but to get warm and obtain a dose of vitamins. We needed tea, hot and quite strong.

Kavunenko decided that the rainy day for which we had kept our most valuable and tasty provisions had arrived and he ordered them brought out "above ground."

"It's not so bleak," said Yura suddenly. "I've seen worse."

"Now Yura!" Kavunenko choked with delight. "There simply aren't words ... We have to be on our guard. Listen, Shatayev, keep an eye on him or he'll grab his ice axe and run off to the summit."

Yura was surprised himself. As often happens, he felt relief immediately—as if the knot that had been squeezing his throat and pinching his blood vessels was untied and the blood was now flowing easily and freely through his veins.

"It's from the smell of the marinated mushrooms," joked Kavunenko. "Wait and see what happens when Shatayev passes the multicolored caviar and opens the herring."

"It seems like a hundred years since I've had your caviar," Piskulov said. "Below we were eager, but you hoarded it. And now ... "

"You see, Yura, it's established: the closer you get to the sky, the more accessible this product is. And your appetite is not in accord with the rules. In medical handbooks it's stated that the selectivity of tastes dries up with altitude; you don't want anything but sour, salty, or hot things."

"You're right." Yura grabbed a lemon and, taking a bite as though from an apple, chewed it without batting an eye.

Our banter was really an expression of worry, all the more so as the bad weather raged on. It seemed that the storm's fury was near a breaking point, after which something frightening would happen, a cataclysm that would carry the mountain down and level the topography. The hysterical howl became higher and higher, turning into a whistle. Every now and then it was covered over by the booming rumble of avalanches.

It took a long time to fall asleep. Toward morning I had nightmares, shapeless and vague. Something heavy, groaning, shouting, pressed on my chest. For some reason I heard Piskulov cry "Stop! Who's that?" I opened my eyes. Impenetrable darkness. All around there was muffled, quilted quiet. It was as if something had seized hold of my throat, stopping my breathing; it seemed I was in a tomb. Having forgotten I was swaddled in a sleeping bag, I tried to raise my hands and became even more frightened. Next to me there was a moan and someone's seemingly breaking, quick, soblike breathing. I remembered that Piskulov was lying next to me. The details of our situation came immediately to mind, and suddenly the thought struck me: we were covered by an avalanche.

Undoing my sleeping bag, I got a match out of my pocket to light a candle. The head had just started to burn when its withered, pale flame went out. I used up half a box of matches before it occurred to me that fire, just like humans, needs oxygen. Somewhere nearby should be a rucksack. At night, before crawling into the bag, I had put a flashlight on it. I found it by feel, lit up the cave, and directed the beam at the entrance. If there had been an avalanche, then the entrance should be obstructed by snow. But it was clean — not a lump of snow. In the doorway the semicircular ledge of a snowdrift jutted out. A blizzard had blocked us in, and we appeared to be locked inside a snow cavity.

A weight had been lifted. It's easier to dig out of a snowdrift than to break through the multi-meter thickness of an avalanche. We would die before we could reach the surface.

I did not wake Piskulov. I shook Kavunenko and we set to the shovels. In a few minutes the snow above us collapsed. A shaft of light and fresh frosty air rushed in through the hole.

An unbearable, merciless whiteness struck us in the face, forcing us to squint. Involuntarily, we reached for our sunglasses. But I could not restrain myself, and before putting them on I glanced at the summit.

The slope where we were was in shadow, but the outline of the ridge was dressed in a blinding, fiery flame with golden knives receding to the west and melting into infinity. At the very top, sparkling with patches of sun, white flags of snow looked deceptively peaceful. Surrounded by a panorama of stout summits and pointed peaks, of the ranges receding into the distance, one felt the morning coolness and the stillness.

My "contemplation" lasted no more than half a minute. Knowing that all this summoned beauty was dangerous, I forced myself to put on my glasses.

A thought about the absurdity of our position suddenly struck me. We go into the mountains of our own free will, but there, as nowhere else, every step is limited, every movement constricted. Even admiring nature is permissible only through dark glasses. But why do we go? After all, nobody forces us; we drag ourselves. Tell Kavunenko now that he cannot go into the mountains for a season and he'll go after you with an ice axe. Why isn't life always logical?

I do understand one thing: such logic only takes the costs

of mountaineering into account. I accept what is secondary to be the main thing. But here it is not the main thing at all. It's that every meter is a struggle and a victory: the more meters, the more victories.

Kavunenko lifted his head and looked upwards, but, so it seemed to me, not at the summit itself. His glasses covered his eyes and I could not follow his gaze. But I guessed by his worried, clouded face what he was looking for. I felt that the thought that had not left me for some time had also occurred to him . . . maybe now, maybe earlier: that somewhere about two hundred meters above us is a place that does not differ from the meters higher up or lower down, a place that turned out to be insurmountable for a climber far stronger than us— Master of Sports Oleg Abalakov, the younger Abalakov. To this day I bow down to his mountaineering talent; I love this man.

I had told myself many times that this place marks his personal, individual threshold. Even with all his climbing skills and robust health, his body does not respond well to high altitude. Other climbers have passed this place without noticing it, without remembering him, and climbed to the summit. There is no objective point to overcome, although it is thought that there is a critical range of altitude, from 6,500 to 7,200 meters. And everyone has his own critical mark there. If that is so, then judging by everything, I had already passed mine.

I said all this to myself, convinced myself of it, but in vain. The example of the younger Abalakov made me anxious.

I started mountaineering when Oleg Abalakov was already well known and respected. People talked about him as about a rising luminary and expected him to exceed his father. He scaled vertical walls, overhangs, and chimneys like a virtuoso, with the precision of a master, beautifully, inspirationally, and even dashingly. His skill, feeling, carefulness, and stinginess with resources not only brought recognition but also aroused open delight.

His climbing tactics were captivating, like a book with an intriguing plot. One thinks there is only one possible way to pass a certain two or three meters on a cliff: to the right is a very reliable foothold, above a protrusion, and here, right at hand, fate has sent an excellent crack for a peteled hook. And when the hook goes in, you think that's the way—the only way. But Oleg cannot stand simple routes. His rare mountaineering sight helps him find what others do not find. He carries out a stunning move, reliably and without guesswork. He moves to the right, using that hold, and like a pendulum flies across to a tiny ledge that nobody took into account because of the great stretch required to reach it.

He amazed us not only as a climber. Oleg is one of those multi-talented individuals who enters every field on a white horse, for whom everything comes easily, quickly, without effort. Somehow he picked up a guitar, having never held one before, touched the strings, and right then and there picked a melody, found a harmony to it, and after half an hour began to play as if he had known the instrument his whole life.

Some people accuse him of immodesty. I have never agreed with them, although outwardly there are grounds for such opinions. If he had behaved differently, I would have been the first to accuse him of insincerity. However, none of these opinions bothers him. I like that in him. It's strange that people would bear a grudge against an intelligent, talented person with a strong, masculine capacity for knowing his own worth and considering it unnecessary to hide it in order to falsely and sanctimoniously pass himself off as a modest person. Such a person knows well that he can do what many others cannot, that he has the right to take on what others cannot touch. He never overemphasizes this necessity, but neither is he ever ashamed to talk about it openly.

Oleg is an excellent person, and the ethics of mountaineering come to him as easily as everything else. I would not think twice whether to be on the same rope with him.

However ... (I say this now, eight years after the climb I am describing here) if I had suddenly been told that he had given up climbing, I would have been happy for him with all my heart. Why?

In this person's character, in his mind, there are none of the scruples and suspicions that at times are excessive in more ordinary individuals who have experienced a life full of toil and difficulties. He has no such experience. He does not know what it means to do something that is useless, to "blow on something already cold." An excess of this quality is not acceptable in mountaineering, but it has to be present to some degree in a climber's character. Then it will crop up to a sufficient degree in stressful situations during an assault.

A "split personality" occurs, one that is a meticulous, tedious, nagging inspector. It analyzes every step, every move, every action. It forces one to listen to oneself as a hypochondriac does. I'm afraid that Oleg is completely lacking in this attribute, unlike his father, Vitaly Abalakov, who has been taken as the standard with respect to it. Although Oleg is a complete master at the technique of belaying, understands in his mind its decisive nature, and has enough will power to force himself to do self-belays, he is not safe enough. This is the single flaw in his mountaineering talent. But it is enough to justify calling him a fatalist.

On level ground one could easily attribute such misadventures to chance. There, one need not, cannot, and does not have reason to think about each and every step.... But for the very reason that risks lie in wait at every meter in the mountains, our ideal of mountaineering mastery, its highest criterion, consists of completing a climb and escaping tens of thousands of such hazards. And still, such things can happen to any of us, precisely because we are all far from the mountaineering ideal. Only a few come close to what has become the living standard for us, close to the older Abalakov, the world-famous climber, the number-one mountaineer in the country, the first to climb Peak Pobeda and many other summits.

I knew and understood all this. And still I doubted that I would pass where Oleg had not succeeded.

Kavunenko looked straight at me and grinned insidiously. Then he turned his gaze to the side, wrinkled up his face, imitating a strained expression, as if deciding an important question, and said, "Should be closed."

"Close what?"

"That." He motioned with his head in the direction of the summit. "The peak. Since Oleg didn't make it once, there's nothing at all for others to do here!"

"Mind reader! You're reading my thoughts. Most likely you're thinking the same."

But he suddenly started to speak seriously and openly. "I'm thinking. And I'm getting angry. We're behaving like schoolkids. Masters of Sports! Athletes' bodies, dystrophic minds! Not a step by ourselves! We're all looking for a precedent and looking toward our neighbors. Okay." He pointed up. "We'll see up there."

"It's all true. Only not there, but here. We need to throw 'neighbor' out of our heads. It will be too late up there. In '33 on Chomolungma Smythe also was thinking about Mallory."

Wind, cold, altitude, topography—these are not all a climber struggles against. There are more difficult obstacles—they exist only in the climber's own head.

2. Oleg Abalakov's "Threshold"
(1968)

During the night the wind had blown on this mountain we were tilting at. The slope we were on was free of loose snow, and under our feet was a thin, smooth, asphaltlike, tightly compacted layer. Our crampons held well and we did not use the picks on our ice axes. We cut fewer than ten steps from 7,000 meters to the summit. Here and there we even found shallow depressions powdered with shifting snow, and the twisted crests of snowdrifts stood on end above the rocks.

Physically it became easier for us. But our concentration became more intense, as our path lay across crevasses. We moved carefully, even by mountaineering standards, using ice-axe belays: wrapping the rope around the shaft, we pulled it against the pick itself.

And still we moved quickly. We changed leads every two or three forty-meter rope-lengths and in an hour gained about a hundred and twenty meters of altitude.

Suddenly it appeared before me, as if just formed: a bright snakelike strip of settled snow. Lengthwise, it stretched about forty meters up the slope and was about a meter wide. I poked at it with my ice axe. The axe slipped in up to the head. Kavunenko and Piskulov stopped where they were and did not approach me. Such are the rules of safety.

Oleg Abalakov's "Threshold" (1968)

Kavunenko put the rope across his axe and drove it into the firn with several strong blows. I did not look around or watch him do it; I only heard the sound of hammer blows. I was calm about how reliable the belay was. Kavunenko is one of those indivuals for whom this work never becomes a bothersome, monotonous, routine obligation. He beats in a belay anchor or ties a knot, always keeping it fresh in his mind that a life is hanging from that anchor or knot.

I jumped across the crevasse and belayed Kavunenko and Piskulov. The crevasse was not at all difficult, but that's not the point. How did it happen that I noticed it only at the last moment? Why hadn't I seen it before? It's true that a minute earlier the edge of the sun came out from behind the summit skyline, not so much blinding as distracting me. But that's no excuse. Afterwards they would say, "A misfortune, chance..." Down on the Bivouac Glacier there were more crevasses, unforeseen and masked over. I saw every last one of them there, for there I was calm and sure that this couldn't happen.

There it is, Oleg Abalakov's threshold—the regularity of altitude where a legion of chances is perceived by the tired brain as an inseparable crowd, where the quantity of mistakes increases, and where the clarity with which one comprehends that any of them could become fatal drops sharply. Now the meaning of this high altitude and high level of confrontation is understandable. Now my intuitive guesses have found a logic: I have come to understand what the strength to overcome this threshold consists of. When you become conscious of it in yourself, then you also realize the capability of reaching the summit: a simple capability to jump, as the Olympic-class highjumper Brumel did, higher than your head, to stand above yourself and to direct your own state of mind from above.

Can I do this, and how? How must it be expressed? How concretely? I know of only one way: to drive myself to the upper limits of psychological effort. To watch every step:

how I place my foot, how I inhale, what's underfoot two meters from myself, five meters, and even twenty-five. I should have seen everything before I made a step.

If a centipede thought about the order in which it placed its legs—which follows which—it couldn't move. But that is a centipede; I have only two feet and still I moved, although I continued to think out every centimeter of progress.

The pace of the group slowed because of me. Nobody said anything, maybe did not think anything, but it was embarrassing. On the other hand, it became clear that high altitude demands just that kind of attention. One must work out precisely such a manner of climbing, or the pace gradually increases.

After an hour the slope began to level off. It stretched out at a moderate angle for about forty meters and then rose sharply. We stopped. The summit looked quite close, but I figured it just seemed that way. Oleg's threshold oppressed me as before: for some reason I was convinced that we had still not crossed it. I decided not to look at the altimeter, but I asked Kavunenko, "Where was he evacuated from?"

Volodya smiled, screwed up his eyes in a sly way, unhurriedly tightened his sleeve, scratched the back of his head through his hood, and suddenly, lifting his ice ace like the conductor of a military orchestra, jerked it sharply and enthusiastically to one side. The spike pointed down. But I still asked, "Have we passed it?"

"Lo-o-ong ago."

I looked at the summit and realized it was quite close. At 4:10 Kavunenko, Piskulov, and I were standing on it, surveying the Pamirs.

Everything else was below us. The earth bristled up in hundreds of peaks. The strange split of consciousness called forth a strange question: Who are we? We're strangers even to ourselves! Now we are those giants for whom the trite thought "Man is master of the world" becomes a real feeling, to whom it seems that to step from summit to summit, to walk about on the planet is a trivial matter. And the weak-sighted ones with their infinitely small view of life, who get tangled up in the threads of their microscopically minute life ...

We started down, and the mountains began to grow above us again. With every step down we felt more and more like small, vulnerable creatures. Our subjective human characteristics—fear, doubt, caution, irritability, egoism, suspiciousness, reliance on others—returned to us with every step, although perhaps in a much smaller degree than we had accumulated on the ground. We began to feel better as we lost elevation, but at the same time we were overtaken by an urgent, vital tension that blocked out the accumulating fatigue, the sleepless nights, the overcooling, and the undernourishment.

The rope worked me into a frenzy. It seemed to be dangling more than usual. I pulled at it and flicked it, adjusting the carabiner through which it passed, and shifted my harness. But it hung as before—it was meant to be so—and caught on an irregularity in the snow. I was ready to get rid of it altogether, but remembered that I was descending. To do such a thing is exactly like walking in heavy traffic for several kilometers.

In the cave at 6,600 meters we met a reconnaissance group of four Ukrainian climbers. Among them were our acquaintances Boris Sivtsov from Donetsk and Vadim Sviridenko from Odessa. The fellows congratulated us on our ascent and offered us tea. It turned out that somewhere below was a large Ukrainian expedition under the leadership of Vladimir Monogarov.

We did not sit long. After half an hour we continued our descent, having decided to bivouac at 6,200 meters.

We had not even left the cave when we met still another group: three members of the Spartak sports society from Kiev. We exchanged a few words and went our separate ways, they up and we down. One of them shouted after us that Asya Klokova had stayed at 6,200. A pleasant meeting awaited me; Asya is a close friend of my wife, Elvira.

Approaching the Peak Pravda plateau, we saw a small figure in a blue anorak with the hood pushed back who was standing by the cave entrance and waving at us. Kavunenko hurried. He had a keen sense of smell, and he said, "If we hurry, we'll be just in time for dinner."

"Now don't be impudent," the delicate Yura worried.

"Okay, okay, I won't."

It was warm inside the cave. The stove was roaring and the pot lid shook intermittently, letting out intoxicating smells that made our heads spin.

Volodya flared his nostrils, drew in air, and closed his eyes in bliss. "Soup! Yugoslavian," he said with a weakening voice.

"But you just had dinner—up at 6,600," Piskulov asserted.

"No, Yura. It was you and Volodya who ate. And you even ate my portion because I refused to and drank only tea," Kavunenko answered affectedly. We could not hold it in and started laughing.

"It's for you," Klokova said. "I noticed you a long time ago. I guessed it had to be you, or, more accurately, I figured it out."

I asked why she had remained there. Had she gotten sick? Asya gave a wry laugh and did not answer immediately.

"After all, I'm a woman. And a woman isn't allowed on a military ship; she's an evil talisman. They didn't take me with them so that I wouldn't bring bad luck."

They had climbed to the Peak Pravda plateau as a group of four: three men and a woman. Klokova had not thrust herself on them. The group as such had been established long before leaving for the mountains, and not one of its members had had any objections to this particular woman participating. And understandably so: Klokova is the strongest female climber in the Ukraine and by rights can be considered the leader of Ukrainian women mountaineers. She had been preparing intensely for this climb all year and was to become the first woman to climb the Peak of Communism.

On the way to the Peak Pravda plateau Asya felt that there had been talk behind her back, discussions. Finally, there at the plateau, it had been suggested that she remain. The others did not give any kind of explanation; they simply announced it as a group decision.

There were no explanations because there was nothing to explain. I have seen her on climbs and I know that she will not fall behind, will not let you down when belaying, and will definitely walk as an equal of the men, not permitting any kind of allowances or indulgences on her account. I know her principles, since she and my wife share them. Nothing will force them to follow the tracks of a preceding group, not even a threat to life. They will wait until the tracks melt. We, male climbers, laughed at such punctiliousness. Elvira's answer to that was always, "They say it is not for men to understand that a woman, all her life, is forced to prove her true equality. In a woman's heart there is a constant desire to convince others that a woman's competence is not less than that of a man. And in mountaineering, women are not parasites, but equals as climbers."

Those who make this last claim would be right about everything if they were right about the main thing, about the equality of female and male tenacity in life. I think there are many things in modern life that would be more perfect if the word "emancipation" were properly interpreted, if it did not drag behind it distorted views of reality, displacement of accents arranged by life itself, and acceptance of what is desired as reality. Unfortunately, mountaineering is a suitable item for the female game of being men.

I will make a stipulation, however. I am not at all against women going into the mountains. On the basis of experience I have come to the conclusion that one must look realistically at the correlation of strengths, at women's possibilities in this type of sport.

I can understand those fellows to some extent. Klokova was the first woman to climb the Peak of Communism. How did she behave? What is the limit of her abilities, even if she is the strongest of the best? Besides that, in such a small group, where each person must break a quarter of the trail and lift a quarter of the weight of the equipment, a woman complicates things both physically and morally. The group is faced with a choice: either divide the fourth person's responsibilities (or at least part of them) among three persons, thereby adding to the already heavy loads, or permit the woman to work as an equal, weighing the whole path down with male shame. (I am only suggesting motives that led the group to that action. The real reasons are not known to me.)

After dinner we left the cave and suddenly heard voices coming from the bend where the slope steepens. Rope team after rope team appeared on the plateau. It was Vladimir Monogarov's Ukrainian expedition.

There were a lot of them, about thirty-five. They walked triumphantly, eyes fixed in front of them, not noticing us. The strongest were in the front of the column, with unrolled banners.

I thought it would have been better to unroll the banners on the summit, to travel the slopes not with a ceremonious step, but with that of a mountaineer, and to conserve strength in order to reach the summit.

Klokova grabbed me by the sleeve and nodded in the direction of two approaching figures. I looked carefully and realized they were women. They walked by without greeting us. Perhaps they did not notice...

Asya suddenly bent over, as if straightening the string on her jacket, then turned sharply and went into the cave. Maybe she had decided that one of the main goals of that expedition was to get women to the summit of the Peak of Communism.

We returned to the cave. Asya, having seen us, stealthily hid her handkerchief. But you cannot hide moist red eyes. Kavunenko, capable of relieving a situation without minimizing or avoiding a touchy subject, but bringing it out into the open, said loudly, without a shadow of a doubt that he was doing the right thing, "Where's your strength of character? Did it all go into the handkerchief? Then let's squeeze it out, pour the strength onto the ground."

"If you were in a woman's shoes—maybe then you would understand."

"I understand women. I'm also an ambitious person, but I don't aspire to the throne of a Nepalese king."

"Facts don't convince you. You point-blank do not see them."

"Precisely. Tell us about Joan of Arc and Sofia Kovalevskaya. Only put this in your pipe and smoke it: history has allowed an incident in which a lady became a colonel, but not yet one in which she became a blacksmith."

"We'll see what you say in a few days when those two come down from the summit!"

"Those two?" He burst out in an emphatic laugh. "They wouldn't make it to the summit even with someone else's efforts. Do you want me to set your mind at rest? Then listen. You could climb the Peak of Communism—you, Shatayeva, Rozhalskaya, or two or three others, no more. In a strong male group, in good weather, and with special preparation. But this does not mean your ascent would open up the road to the summit for women. Because it would be no more than a record forced by a whole crowd. What's bad is that afterwards any badge carrier would consider it the norm and would start flapping her wings in order to flit up to seven and a half thousand. You try very hard to stand on an equal footing with men in everything. But emancipation is equality of rights, not of capabilities."

"Okay, Volodya, thank you for the compliment. But I think we are not five, but a whole legion."

"I know your legion. Every woman down below is contemporary. She doubts the old truths with Einstein's daringness. 'Who says,' she says, 'that men are stronger than I? It's said that it's not a matter of muscle. I make up for it: I'm more patient and stronger in character.' That's down there. But up here, when the altitude and bad weather close in, she quickly remembers: 'Oh! I'm only a weak woman. I don't have the strength to fight; I'll stay here!' "

"But I know men who behave the same way at high altitude."

"There are some. But you are the first to say about such people, 'not a man, but an old woman.' And the opposite about women: 'as they say, what can you do—a woman!' "

There was no end to this argument. I decided to turn the conversation to another topic, since a good idea had come to mind: to climb Peak Pravda all together, and in this way at least to somehow rectify Klokova's insulting situation. We had time. We had returned three days ahead of schedule. The fellows supported me readily. Only Asya, suspecting it was being done for her, started to object.

"Only without any sacrifices," she said. "I don't accept sacrifices."

Kavunenko stretched, feigned a yawn, and said through his yawning, "As you wish. Then stay here; wait for us. We're starting off for Peak Pravda early tomorrow morning. The summit is beautiful. Why not go?"

Peak Pravda rises only 300 meters above the plateau. The summit is not technically difficult. The next day, leaving camp at dawn, we climbed it and were back by evening.

We let Klokova take the lead often so that she would have stronger impressions of the climb. And it appeared not to be in vain—her mood improved.

We had just returned to the cave when Monogarov's expedition appeared again on the plateau. Only they were not moving so triumphantly and were without banners.

Kavunenko was surprised. "Rather early. Even earlier than I thought. Most likely they didn't even reach seven thousand."

This time they stopped. Many of them came over to us,

including Vladimir Monogarov. True to form, Kavunenko said to Monogarov, "You remind me of Napoleon," and added, "after the Russian campaign."

"Just try getting to seven and a half with such a crowd," Monogarov answered.

"It's not a matter of that. You simply confused the slopes of the Peak of Communism with Kreshchatik Street. Only the gods lead parades up to the summit. And that is on Olympus. Is it actually a summit? It's a pimple!"

Monogarov is a talented, experienced climber. He knew as well as we did that the slopes of the highest summit in the country are not the place for performances. To this day I cannot understand how such a thing could have happened in a group he was leading. I will say with confidence, however, that it was not on his own initiative. But one should not give in so easily to the desires of others, especially when they are less competent.

Climbing, like everything else, has its deficiencies, narrow places, problematic knots. Many who come here view it too practically, expecting some sort of material gain. They give rise to many unpleasant events in our field. Fortunately, the higher the class of climbing, the more it is cleansed of these events. On the other hand, the complexity of the relations between climbers, the competitive channel so to speak, increases. In serious climbing this "channel" is sufficiently great. But nothing is left of it on the climbs themselves: the more skillful the master, the more developed in him the readiness to sacrifice in difficult situations for the sake of a friend. If it is otherwise, then it is completely wrong. Later I will touch on such cases, even if only to prove the rule by the exceptions. Now I will talk about the negative aspects of climbing, which are most characteristic in the world of lower-class climbers. For this I will return to the beginning of my climbing career.

3. The Mountain Sickness: "Ratingomania" (1957–1958)

My involvement in sports came late and unexpectedly. Until the tenth grade, I reacted to sports with decided indifference. I did not like physical-education classes, avoided them whenever possible, and at times even escaped them. Fellows who were literally crazy about sports reacted to the classes in roughly the same way. A good half of the class involved sections devoted to boxing, wrestling, fencing, and gymnastics. It's incomprehensible: sports attract young people, but when made into a school subject, lose their appeal for some reason.

Exercises were required for which I, like many others, was not prepared. Several times, hanging helplessly on a gymnastics apparatus, I amused the class. After that I fully believed in my ineptitude in sports.

"No, there's no need, and I don't want to!"—the road along which pride led me, a road leading to the conviction that it is more attractive and interesting to develop one's intellect than one's body. In short, the usual youthful "either/or." But the actual situation was different: though not attracted by any physical education section taught at school, on my own I skied with pleasure in winter, and in summer I never crawled out of the water and could swim rather well.

At the beginning of tenth grade, the school for some reason conducted a race. Our class put together a team, and while discussing the candidates someone said in jest "Shatayev!" The friendly, open laughter stung me to the quick. I do not remember how, but I got my way and got on the team.

The next day I took second place in the 800-meter race. Can it be that pride is the main talent in sports?

Afterwards came the regional competition for students. And there I finished in the top three. Then I joined the track-and-field section of the Voluntary Sports Society—Spartak. I was active for six years (1955–1960) and several times took prize-winning place in All-Union championships. During that period I also received the first rank in skiing and the second in shooting and bicycling.

I have intentionally omitted the events that brought me to climbing so that I could talk about them in more detail now. There were three of us besides my mother: an older brother, an older sister, and me. Our father had died at the front. My mother had been a housewife while he was alive, but having no specialty, she now worked as a yardwoman. There was no other choice.

We lived in the center of Moscow. We had no subsidiary income, and therefore lived with great difficulty. To lessen the family's burden, my mother accepted an aunt's invitation and every year sent me to Kislovodsk [in the Caucasus] for summer vacation.

I saw the mountains for the first time when I was twelve. The impressions remain to this day. I will say only that at that time, the first night, I jumped out of bed half-conscious, like a sleepwalker, crawled out through the window into the garden, and looked spellbound at the black walls with lily-white tops that had lost their contours and dissolved in the moonlight.

The local boys did not share my rapture: "Stones and more stones and snow on top" is natural for people who from birth are used to a mountain landscape. But later I was convinced that they were only indifferent to a view that had calloused the eye. If they approached the mountains, they too looked with emotion at the nature surrounding them.

I succeeded in enticing new friends for walks into the mountains. And even though they were not allowed out of the house willingly, in the course of five summers we rummaged through almost half the environs of Kislovodsk.

We did not walk aimlessly, but "on business." The business consisted of searching for rare shale, odd stones, minerals, and cockleshells in lime beds and hunting for bright butterflies. We photographed the mountain scenery and admired nature, not shying away from vocal delight.

Wherever we went my eyes inevitably came to rest on Elbrus, the snow-covered mass that seemed like Gulliver, even against the background of the Caucasian colossi. In the evening its double head turned blue and I had the sweet dream of seeing it under my feet.

When I was a little older I considered it a realistic, obtainable objective. During my last vacation, before entering tenth grade, I decided to try my luck.

I did not have the slightest understanding of climbing; and I did not even realize this ignorance. I thought myself to be at home in the mountains. The only thing I had sufficient brains to realize was not to go alone. That meant I had to find a companion.

Prosaists are as rare at seventeen as romantics are at fifteen. Seventeen is the age of paradoxes: when judgment is too concrete but dreams and goals are too abstract; when your own future seems too unusual but for the time being you are living and acting too ordinarily; when you are too quick in desires and too slow with the hand. At seventeen you do and feel everything in extremes.

There were no prosaists among my Kislovodsk friends. At

The Mountain Sickness: "Ratingomania" (1957–1958)

least they did not seem so at first glance. Everyone I introduced to my idea not only understood and respected it but was even caught up in the fire of it. The fire burned as long as the idea did not take on concrete dates: a week for preparation, and we'll set off on such and such day, at such and such time. Then the question arose: Will Ivan go? "If Ivan does, then I will too." And Ivan, as it happened, was referring to Petr. In short, selecting an "expedition" turned out to be not an easy matter. Sympathizers were many, willing ones... alas... Perhaps for such an endeavor it is not enough to be just a romantic; one must be at least a little reckless.

I still managed to find a companion.

Eric was also from Moscow. Like myself, he came every summer to relatives in Kislovodsk. Reserved, even closed, he kept his distance most of the time and preferred a book to many of our ventures. Unexpectedly, he accepted my proposal.

We set off with puny rucksacks and equipment with which even a hiker on a group trip to the outskirts of Moscow would not venture. We had, understandably, neither mountain boots nor comfortable clothes, not to mention ropes, carabiners, or ice axes. We even managed to forget matches. When we suddenly remembered, the city was behind us. It was a good thing that an old mountain man came across us—he came to our aid, donating two boxes. The old man said there were wolves and bears in the area and, most important, dangerous people.

We were not frightened, but our confidence was removed as if by the wave of a hand. Having broken off walking sticks from a tree, we were now walking more carefully and not so fast. Now I know that the foothills of Elbrus are more difficult, more impassable, than the mountain itself—the summit is technically easy. Almost all the routes on Elbrus are no higher than the second degree of difficulty. ([In the Soviet Union] mountaineering routes are divided into six degrees of difficulty, each of which, except the last, is split into subcategories *a* and *b*. Subcategory *a* is the simpler one. The last degree, the highest, does not have subcategories.)

Elbrus is insidious for those who are unfamiliar with the effects of high altitude in general, or for leaders who do not take an altitude of 5,633 meters seriously, thinking a peak of that height can be taken on the run without acclimatization. But for the competent climber this mountain is not difficult.

We did not understand then that the most difficult part of the job was to approach the base of the mountain, particularly by our route. After all, we tried our utmost not to deviate from a visual straight line.

Our hearts would not tolerate going a roundabout way. Cutting off the road, we clambered up steep slopes of spurs overgrown with bushes and descended into ravines, forcing our way through thick, high grasses. The flushed winged creatures hung around persistently, stinging, biting, and tickling. Finally, frightened by the gadflies, horseflies, and wasps, torn by thorns, lashed by branches, we walked out onto the bank of the Malka.

The river raged, foamed, and roared so angrily and aggressively that it was scary even to think about crossing it.

Terrible! But even more terrible was to admit this to each other.

Eric, dirty, spotted with sticking cobwebs, gray from fatigue and fear, tried to tell me something. But his voice was drowned out by the din. You could only see his lips moving—you could not hear sounds, not even shouts.

About seventy kilometers of travel were behind us. Our hearts had sunk to our boots. Shouldn't we go back now? All the same, we did not fully understand the danger, or we would not have gone on.

Now I am not even struck by the fact that we decided on this move. It's understandable: our youthful fear of looking like cowards was stronger. I am amazed at our luck. To overcome this river without a belay, without any knowledge of methods of crossing—success was one chance in ten!

The Mountain Sickness: "Ratingomania" (1957–1958)

We crossed the Malka twice, over and back. We found a quieter spot and, without any incident, reached our goal along a row of boulders that were unstable and not always suitable for jumping.

When we finally reached the foot of the mountain the romantic fog in our brains had dispersed. But our climber's passion did not lose its grip. We were ready to go to the top, only now we viewed the matter as adults: without equipment, without a food supply or the necessary strength, exhausted by what we had already covered, we were not to reach the summit. We discussed the situation openly and candidly and decided it was also no small matter to reach the glacier.

We did succeed in that—not a step more and not a step less. We touched the glacier with our hands. Trimmed by the moraine deposits, it receded into the distance and disappeared behind a bend in the cliffs. All that smoke-gray melancholy was irrepressibly attracting. Looking at the tongue of the glacier, we made a vow that in the next five to six years, as soon as we started independent lives, we would climb Elbrus.

We returned home feeling the trip had been a victory. There was nothing more we could have done, with coats of "fish fur" on our shoulders, zero experience behind us, and half-empty rucksacks. The single thing we feared was that our friends in Kislovodsk would not understand and consider the success a defeat.

o

Five years passed. All those years I was involved in track and field. And I lived as though I did not actually leave the running track for a second. I spent every passing day with the growing tension of a runner, with a persistent passion that made it impossible and impermissible to pause, even for a minute, to catch my breath. I lived carelessly, not stopping for a second to look around, to digress from tactics, and to think about my life strategies. I passed the days week after week and month after month from training to competition, from competition to training. During breaks and transitions I thought about the failure of the day's race, or the reverse, and what I had to do in conjunction with this in the next day's activities. During all this time there was not one hour of calm and balance. I was always suffering from something —now success, now failure. They say that artists live this way. Probably. But the life of most athletes follows this pattern. I remember that on New Year's Eve, 1957, I went to bed a little earlier, at nine o'clock, so that I would sleep better and be at training fresh and cheerful in the morning.

I don't know whether my withdrawal from track and field was the result of a transition I had been undergoing for many years or not, but it happened not long after, in early 1958, that I happened to read an announcement at Spartak. The announcement said that the mountaineering section was selling passes to the Shkhelda climbing camp in the Caucasus. I stopped there and looked around. I thought about my possibilities in track and field. I felt that their limit was near, that they were coming to an end, and that the prophecy of trainers, who had promised me laurels on the running track, was not justified. I boast only that I was never mistaken in this account and had realized rather quickly what I was capable of. Many of my sports friends trained less but attained more. I am sober in my self-evaluation and I could not be deceived either by the delusions of the trainers or by the compliments of friends. I knew that my innate talent would hardly let me advance beyond the first rank. But this in no way had influenced my working mood—I had worked at full output because I loved sports and was carried away by them.

I decided to inquire about the announcement. I also remembered the vow made at the glacier. It seemed naive to me. But I thought, If vows are not fulfilled, it is often because people consider themselves smarter today than they were yesterday, for having remembered the given words, they think, "How naive I was!"

The Mountain Sickness: "Ratingomania" (1957–1958)   41

The cost of the pass turned out to be small, and since I was now an independent person—I worked and earned money—it was reasonable.

In the lobby of the building where I went to see about the announcement, two men were looking through a photograph album. I asked how to find the mountaineers. One of them, not very tall, with sandy-colored, slightly wavy hair, looked at me cheerfully and said, "Mountaineers? I think at the very top. What do you think?" he turned to his companion. The latter pursed his lips, holding back a laugh. I thanked him and was about to go, but he stopped me. "Wait," he said, "let's look together." We approached a room. He opened the door, nudged me ahead, and, standing behind me, asked those sitting at a desk, "How do you get to Everest?"

Up to the present I have not yet followed the path to Everest, but with the help of this man I plunged into climbing. At the time I could not appreciate my luck—how was I to know that, straight off, fate had bumped me into one of the fathers of Soviet mountaineering, the well-known climber (both in our country and abroad) Mihail Ivanovich Anufrikov.

When they say "Anufrikov" lovers of mountaineering recall his climbs to the Caucasian summit Chan-Chahi (in the Tsejsky district), to Ulutau-Chana, to the famous Mazarskie tops in the Pamirs—the traverse of Muzdzhilga-Sandal, one of the first traverses of the legendary Ushba, and many others. Experts in the history of mountaineering will call these climbs contributions, landmarks, events, happenings, and many other words that are perhaps worn out but exact in their meaning.

Anufrikov's pedagogic talent, it seems to me, is connected with the main trait of his character or, more likely, is a result of it—he is kind. Not the type of kindness that people sometimes take as a lack of character, but that strict, perhaps even at times severe kindness that comes from a subtle understanding of human nature, from not being indifferent toward people but rather from a concern for them.

He was stern in his evaluations of my growth as a mountaineer. He reacted to success in a reserved way and did not look for words to sober me if they turned my head. After five years, when I had completed the norm for Master of Sports, he said, "It's true. The statistical time from badge holder to Master is eleven years. But if you jump for joy for the remaining six years, then you will jump from Master to badge holder."

Anufrikov is a virtuoso climber. But no two virtuosos are alike. One, reaching a professional height, intuitively prepares things delicately and scents the nuances of the profession. But it does not occur to him to interpret his ability so subtly, to think where it comes from, to search it out according to some principle, some regularity, some system. He knows how, but he is clearly unable to explain why. The need to realize this does not arise in him.

Others are analysts of their own ability. They examine their experience and find the main thing—a method. They are not simply masters, they are methodists. It is natural that they are bursting with the desire to give movement to the method, to teach others.

Anufrikov taught me that a smart climber climbs to the summit three times. The first time is with his eyes—looking at a detailed map of the route, learning its dangers by heart, considering all that nature might have in store, predicting and imagining possible difficulties. Only after this can he undertake the physical ascent. Having returned home, he must climb once again to the summit—sitting in a chair, reliving the whole route step by step, with all its details.

I was convinced of the truth of his words. The climber who does not follow this method is left with a nominal count of summits reached but with many large gaps in experience, for at high altitude thinking is too restricted and even the simplest and most concrete generalizations and conclusions do not always come to mind. If you get away with a mistake, you sometimes do not notice it then. Therefore, disregarding the fact that all the ascents I have attempted up to this time have led me to the summit, I have not added even one defeat to my score. In the "chair," in hindsight, I have broken out in a cold sweat more than once as I remembered severe, particularly "evil" moments. On the slopes they were either misunderstood or unnoticed. But later, when I thought through the climb step by step, it would suddenly come to me: if it were not for chance, I would have had to part with the mountains forever.

Someone once advised Anufrikov to be more circumspect in giving out passes to novices, particularly to women—they come to the camp, this person said, to find a husband. "May God make them happy!" he answered. "Good for them! They procure marriage by means of fortitude!"

Anufrikov always has his movie camera along on trips. At times he takes pictures in the most difficult and impossible conditions. Friends joke, "God save him if he flies into an abyss; he'll certainly take pictures as he falls." For us his films were a learning aid. The film of the traverse in the Pamirs of Muzdzhila-Sandal became a primer for those who were learning the science of climbing. Even now, having my own experience, I often run through some of his films before leaving for the mountains.

I have noticed more than once that this type of sport scares many people away with its apparent inaccessibility. It seems to them that one has to be particularly athletic even to take the first step. But it is not so. Anyone who has reason to expect a medical certificate of normal health can get a badge and even the third rank.

I too started with caution in my heart, although everything seemed easier for me than others. Instruction started from ground zero, with things that, it seemed to me at the time, did not need to be learned: how to put on clothes and shoes. Experience was developed gradually and logically. In Moscow, long before our departure for the Caucasus, I practiced pounding in pitons, tying knots, making steps, setting up a tent, digging a cave, packing a rucksack, and using a stove. I became acquainted with medicine, cartography, ways of crossing cliffs, ice and snow, means of descent, crossing rivers, and mountaineering terminology. In short, when I arrived at the climbing camp I already knew something, I was capable of something.

I liked the camp from the first day, and up to the last was not bored. Not only because we had sports facilities at our disposal: a pool, a tennis court, volleyball and basketball courts. And not only because there were movies and dances. But because there was as much as one could want of something else, the most important thing—contact with people, humor, and laughter.

Miraculously, the camp eliminates the variables of age: the forty-year-olds act as mischievously and naughtily as the seventeen-year-olds. On the first morning, having woken up, I threw my feet into my slippers out of habit. But in the place where I had left them the night before, there were crampons. My neighbors were hurrying me, seriously and anxiously. "Get dressed," they said, "or we'll be late." Then Boris Tsidelkovsky, a thirty-seven-year-old writer of jokes, said in astonishment, "A real mountaineer! He opened his eyes, threw his crampons on his bare feet, and he's off to the summit at a run—to mix the pleasant with the necessary."

Perhaps this characteristic of the camp is a small part of the infinitely long and not even very clear answer to the age-old question, What is the basis of climbing? What is its essence? Why do people go into the mountains? I have asked myself and my colleagues these questions many times, and I have come to a conclusion: one can collect their opinions like stamps or coins.

"For my health," say some. "From the esthetic need to enjoy nature's beauties," explain others. "From an innate passion for adventure," jokes a third group. "Self-examination, self-affirmation," answers a fourth group. And all are right in their way.

But it seems to me that all this does not explain the hopeless, incurable "alcoholism" from which people suffer when suddenly the mountains suit them body and soul. Eventually such people get into big messes, and despite their atheism, they pray like pagans to all the gods to help get them out, promising never to come again. But just as soon as the February winds die down and the March sun rolls out like a signal, the mountains become the main character in their recurring dreams. Then there is no more pleasurable activity for them than to watch the snow thaw and the tear-off calendar become thinner with the removal of each passing day.

Not one of them can say what the force is that draws them to the mountains.

"We go because it draws us." But why does it? What is the source of this drive? More than once I have wondered why it is that the higher a civilization, the more developed the climbing and the more popular it becomes.

The sources of climbing go back to ancient history. However separate and extremely rare ascents were—literally a handful distributed over centuries—they cannot be taken as mere accidents. Even so, mountaineering with its methodology, system, traditions, popularity, and philosophy is the property of our century, and particularly of the last four to five decades. And not the least of all because new technical possibilities for its development have appeared with civilization. Pitons, ropes, ice axes, and the rest of the basic technology of climbing—these constitute the so-called main condition of the game.

Moreover, the mass attraction to this type of sport grows most of all in the more developed countries: here in the Soviet Union, where hundreds of thousands of persons are attracted to mountain climbing; in the countries of Europe; in the United States; in Japan. The climbing club in Japan, for example, numbers more than half a million persons. It would not be correct to attribute this to the topography of the Japanese islands. It is known that local inhabitants of mountain regions are the least susceptible to the passions of mountaineering.

Then why? You cannot give any one answer to this question....

Civilized man has indeed sat too long. He gets his daily bread not with the help of a hammer and anvil or a bargeman's strap, but more and more with the help of a button and a cylinder.... In many countries, not making full use of individuals' physical abilities will become all but a national problem.

And here lies the thirst for strong feelings, a thirst that many of us are guilty of having. A thirst all the more likely as life becomes protected, securely level, and even oppressively insipid for some. Perhaps some hereditary trait causes the feelings to begin searching for an exit—a trait from our cave forefathers, from those who went out against a mammoth with stones in their hands and who, even in their sleep, kept one eye open in case of danger.

A person in the mountains seems to get to know himself faster. He learns things about himself that as a rule he does not succeed in discovering in conditions of warmth, satiety, and reliable shelter. It is known that the higher the level of culture in a person, the more he is disposed to self-analysis. Mountains are a good basis for testing strengths. Reaching the summit, people are happy not because they struggled with the rock and conquered it but because they struggled with and conquered themselves. It is seductive to obtain this right to self-respect and confirm it.

But all this, of course, far from exhausts the explanations. I would like to hope that this book will provide, at least in some degree, an answer to the question of why people climb.

o

The Mountain Sickness: "Ratingomania" (1957–1958)

The crampons that had replaced my slippers belonged to somebody else. I received my own the same day in lineup after exercises, and in addition a rucksack, an ice axe, carabiners, mountain boots. This was sufficient to make me feel like a climber. But another two years were necessary for me to understand how far I was from being a real mountaineer.

We spent about five days on the cliffs, practicing on grassy slopes and scree. On the eve of a real trip to the mountains—this time it would begin where the glacier started—I painstakingly rubbed my boots with glacier oil, prepared my rucksack, and went to bed. It was still early. I did not fall asleep quickly and I slept restlessly. At nine o'clock in the morning we were walking in the direction of the river Adylsu. On our shoulders we had loads of about twenty-five kilograms—not so much by my standards now.

Mountaineers call the rucksack the main friend and enemy. At that time I related to it one-sidedly, having considered only its hostility. There is sufficient air at this altitude, but we could breathe fully only during ten-minute halts. One more conclusion: it is necessary to learn to breathe with a rucksack on.

Finally, having crossed the Adylsu by a bridge, we found ourselves in a thick, southerly, warm, coniferous forest from which—strange!—a glacier led into the mountains. Ground down, dug out into ditches and channels, it oozed lazily and flowed in puny streams.

We set up our tents, split into twos, and immediately got down to business. I was teamed with Kostya Smirnov (I'll use that name), a long-standing friend of mine from Moscow. It seemed that we had been through thick and thin together, but it did not help. After several hours of practice it became clear that we barely knew each other.

We chopped steps, pounded in pitons, oriented ourselves on the route. For some reason, Kostya immediately took upon himself the role of leader and was such an organizer that Boris Tsidilkovsky came up to him and said, "Kostya, watch yourself. If you keep this up it won't take long for a heart attack to strike."

I had difficulty moving in his steps, which were formless, poorly cleared, small holes; you placed your foot but didn't feel any support. Kostya had immediately revised the classical method and chopped them in his own way. Instead of first cutting the ice with horizontal blows of the axe, he immediately chopped away from above. If an instructor happened to be near, Kostya undertook to teach me how to walk.

We walked around a field of seracs, along a path marked by flags—Smirnov in front, of course. Without consulting me he decided to take a shortcut, to go as straight as possible. He changed the course and led me into an ice thicket that we barely got out of.

"Listen, fellow, in mountaineering, people perish from such habits!" an instructor said, having seen us.

Unfortunately, Kostya continued to be in love with himself. I could not stand it and said more softly, trying not to offend him, "They say it's not worth doing the unnecessary."

"What concern is it of yours?" he answered.

As a matter of fact, does it concern me or not?

Climbers have their own jargon, their own humor, and even an oral "encyclopedia." It says in it, *I:* see *We.* If I have clipped the team rope into my carabiner, that means that *I* and *we* are one and the same concept. From then on I should say "*We* climbed to the summit," "*We* fell," or "*We* are dying." For the sake of the flow of the writing one should interchange the words *mountaineer* and *climber*. But they are not one and the same. A climber becomes a mountaineer when he has accumulated in himself a certain moral quality that operates automatically as soon as he joins a team. Its meaning is understandable. It is not worth explaining—usually it is called a feeling of comradeship. It is, perhaps, the most complex thing of all that a mountaineer must learn.

The Mountain Sickness: "Ratingomania" (1957–1958)

Overhead there is some "cotton padding," completely dirty—gray to be exact—worn down by dampness. You constantly think of it as a half-formed, suspended monster, and you don't know whether it is rain or snow. The wind is gusty and dank; it does not so much chill you as get to your heart and spoil your mood. But this is all tolerable; the main thing is something else.

We are on the way to our first summit. My mountaineering debut has already lasted several hours. I want to catch up to the group, a long row of people loaded down, half bent-over, walking slowly and in silence.

Sometimes someone—most often a woman—steps out of the flow without waiting for a halt and throws herself down in the wet snow so as to gain two or three minutes' rest before the tail of the column comes alongside. The instructors ask, "Are there any who cannot go on?" Everyone is silent.

The summit of Gumachi is already noticeable, even with the present visibility. But there is still one more crossing before we come out on the col. The last fifty meters of the slope become steeper and the order goes to pieces. The steepness, like a filter, sorts the people impassively and mercilessly—the weaker ones fall into the "second echelon." But all come out on the col.

On the small, even ledge forty-five novices are talking. They have not yet experienced the intoxicating feeling of conquering a summit, but they have had an intriguing foretaste.

The instructors are standing to one side, talking quietly about something. Then one of them comes toward us. He raises his hand, expecting attention, and explains, "Your climb ends here. There is nothing for you to do on the summit." Period. No more words, or explanations, or justifications.

Several fellows, keeping to themselves like a small isolated flock and looking as though they had just emerged from a country bath, openly rejoiced at the announcement. I then understood that inner inflexibility is something indestructible, and that not even the mountains are capable of disturbing some people's indifference.

The two instructors climbed to the summit and left a note with a list of members of the climb.

It would seem as if mountaineering should be naturally immune to narrow-mindedness. Unfortunately, some mountaineers are not. That is because people without a germ of a calling fall into every activity, even the most forbidding. When one calling fails to move them, they do not attempt to penetrate its depths, but instead look for other means of self-affirmation. In short, mountaineering is not, unfortunately, immune from inflexibility, from profanation by different types and natures.

On that occasion, those two instructors did a hack job, and not without harmful consequences. They sparked skepticism in the hearts of beginning climbers. What did the novices think after that? What would you think if below, your teachers went on and on about the passion of mountaineering, about its inexplicably mysterious attraction, while up above, they ignored this passion so blatantly?

The impression of months of painful ordeals can be fully blocked out by a momentary experience of victory. But here were only ordeals—it was obvious that many in that group would never again be lured into climbing, not for love nor money.

And in the West there was a climber who had with him some portable mechanism instead of a climbing hammer. The mechanism drilled holes and pounded in bolts. This person climbed smooth slabs effortlessly where it usually takes about 150 strikes of the hammer for every bolt.

He soloed one of the problematic Andean walls and did not break into a sweat. After him the route lost its virgin beauty and took on an openly industrial look—the dodger developed a taste for putting in a bolt every one and a half to two meters, whether it was needed or not.

Of course it is a personal matter—nobody could forbid

The Mountain Sickness: "Ratingomania" (1957–1958)   51

him. It is possible that he did not pretend to call himself a mountaineer. Maybe he simply wanted to go into the mountains, to stand on the summit (if you shut your eyes to the fact that he made it to the summit not just by any route, but by a problematic wall). But I will take the opportunity to say this: such free actions, as they begin to spread, can with time have an influence on the main conditions and principles of mountaineering. That is, whether we like it or not, this simplification through lack of standards will begin to penetrate our sport.

Modern times have already given mountaineering not a few indulgences. Helicopters ever more frequently deliver us to base camp. They sometimes even drop provisions at intermediate bivouacs. This is forgivable inasmuch as it still does not go beyond the bounds of the principles of mountaineering. But if one begins to automize the very process of ascents, then only the name remains of mountaineering. Why don't we ascend in a fireman's automatic ladder, or better yet in an elevator?

This person did not hide it—he used his mechanism openly. But there will be those who begin to use such means secretly, later laying claim to athletic achievements and recognition. In short, there could open up in mountaineering a large breach for charlatanism, resembling what we saw in the case of the instructors. It is worth talking about this. Unfortunately, one meets among climbers people who are attracted not by the summits of mountains but by the summits of athletic careers.

Some climbers, especially in the West, think that in our country this betrayal of mountaineering stems from its being accorded the status of a sport. They think that our system of athletic categories gears mountaineering toward this. It is true: there exists an intermediate moment in one's growth as a mountaineer when one is attracted to climbing the hierarchical stairs no less than climbing mountains. It is understandable and natural—a vivacious person strives toward self-affirmation. But one does not hinder the other: a true athlete, setting off on a route, forgets about practical gains. To reach the summit is the goal, the desire, and the meaning of life—although, of course, it also happens that another, for example a person of the third rating, sees in every conquered meter of the slope nothing more than one more step toward the second rating. But it is not the rating that is to blame. In the West, mountaineering is not considered a sport, and the qualifications of climbers are not divided into ranks (although there they refer to climbers being strongest, strong, satisfactory, novice—you cannot escape it). But if there is no ratingomania there, then it is recordomania. And that is even worse.

Later, in 1964, on one of the complicated and dangerous routes on Grand Kaptsin in Italy, we were passed by two Frenchmen. They were the fastest climbers I'd ever seen, but had almost no margin of safety. The reason their climbing was unsafe was their speed. But how else? They needed a speed record. Looking at them, I thought that one day the Alps would be called the biggest cemetery in Europe...

Once again I will state the known truth: It is characteristic of humans to strive toward self-affirmation. And an athlete canot remain indifferent to glory and prestige. But we are dealing with situations where the athletic career becomes the end in itself and leads to a lack of moral scruples.

Fortunately, mountaineering has a strong self-policing tendency. Individuals with such moral defects seldom succeed in getting further than the second rating. This is easy to explain: It is difficult to conceal oneself on a climb. There a person opens up completely, if not the first time, then the second or the third. Even if people in a group react indifferently to unacceptable behavior—because this one time it is not at their expense—still nature is nature and soon an action that does harm the group will surface. Then, people will say loudly and categorically, "We will not attempt any more summits with this person!" And they will add, "We advise others to do the same."

4. The Brocken-spectra Phenomenon
(1959)

It snowed that night. I settled into the tent, which was warmed by the stove and our warm, living bodies. Nobody had had the sense to surround it with a drainage ditch, and meltwater was flowing underneath us. You could even wring things out.

We passed the night almost without sleep, although we needed it badly—the day before had been difficult and exhausting. The problems had started in the morning. To begin with, we had had to force this climb—the traverse of peaks Vulley and Kavkaz—out of the camp head, Shakir Tenishev. It exceeded the norms, and he had resisted for a long time. After that the person who gives permission—the leader of the rescue team—had examined us carefully. He checked our equipment and quizzed us on our knowledge of the route. He did this so captiously and meticulously that I could not contain myself: "After such a check we need to go to a rest home." I flattered him, he answered.

Then we had gone along a moraine. Sown with huge boulders and debris from the cliffs, it stretched rather steeply to the glacier. It completely exhausted us by forcing us to jump with heavy rucksacks along the rocks. Toward the end we preferred to move along the small, shifting fragments that spurted out from under our feet and went around the blocks.

The glacier was covered with snow. This is its most dangerous condition. But we were glad to reach it, as though we had run into a grassy spot. An economical, careful, rhythmic climber's step on an insidious glacier is better than chaotic movement along an innocent moraine. There, after a day that had ended for us at two in the morning, we put our sleeping spot into order.

The weather destroyed the route we had selected at three o'clock the morning before. The snow was like a thick, swirling dust, not so much settling as moving in the air. Visibility was no more than twenty-five meters. The wind was unpredictable, inconsistent, seemingly blowing with no respite and completely without direction.

Toward eight o'clock it cleared slightly. We moved quickly, harnessed ourselves into our rucksacks, and set off, going to the left along a steep scree slope.

A massif with a palisade of summits rose before us like a puzzle. Which one of them was Peak Vulley? Nobody knew, not even our instructor, Shaliko Margiani. He was guessing, using his fingers to count. Then he decided to go up the first couloir we came across. He said we would check things out there at the top.

We crept up, afraid of our own steps, as if we had gotten into somebody else's garden: a couloir is the place in the mountains with the most rockfall. But Shaliko knew that in such weather it is no more dangerous than any other part of the mountain. The rocks, frozen together, lie firmly in place.

The exit onto the upper skyline did not clarify anything. As everyone knows, there are no signs hanging on summits, and therefore in searching for the cairn we had to traverse about five tops. Ashamed of ourselves, we decided that two of us should go on a reconnaissance. Shaliko and Leva Uspensky threw down their packs and went ahead. Stepanov and I remained.

The weather became worse. The snow dust beat into our eyes and noses and made it difficult to breathe. I wanted to tuck in a lock of hair that had come out from under my wool cap, but having touched it, I jerked my hand back in fear—my own hair buzzed like a wire in damp weather. I had not expected any such thing, and was more surprised than frightened. Stepanov and I quickly cast aside our ice axes and rucksacks—everything that contained metal—and hid in a nearby hollow.

There was a deafening crash of thunder, and the mountain seemed to quiver. It seemed to us that the bolts of lightning were falling stronger and stronger around us, as if shooting at a goal. Stasik counted about five of them that were, he assured me, right next to us.

We were worried about the others. When it quieted down a little, we decided to go look for them, but at that moment they appeared. They had not found the cairn but had left notes on two neighboring towers. In Margiani's opinion, one of them was Peak Vulley.

"Now," said Shaliko, "we will descend to Shkheldinsky Pass, and from there we'll go to Peak Kavkaz."

"Stepanov and I have still not been on Vulley." I was angry. I had the feeling that some kind of unscrupulous, cheap lie was impregnating and poisoning the thing I had dreamed about so much and struggled for so hard. I was here for the second time and for a second time I was suffering a defeat. If I allowed myself to be deceived this time again, then I would be pronouncing the sentence on myself: I would not become a mountaineer.

But I was lucky. The weather calmed immediately, as though someone had turned off powerful fans that had been swirling the air and snow. Visibility improved and it became warmer. Now we had a good view of the slopes, spurs, and ridge outlines crowned by a multitude of summits. Not one of them resembled another; each had its own "face."

Shaliko looked up and suddenly said, "There it is!" It

turned out that the tower next to where we were hiding was Peak Vulley.

Climbing it did not present any difficulties. And we found the cairn. We pulled out the can, took out the note left by the previous climbers, and placed our own in exchange.

We climbed Peak Kavkaz without our rucksacks, which we hid in a convenient place below Shkheldinsky Pass. A steep slope led us out onto a ridge, and here my first self-examination occurred. The ridge, covered with ice and sharp enough so that both feet pressed tightly against each other barely fit, stretched in this way for about two hundred meters. From one look, a feeling of nausea came to my throat and my legs would not obey. To go or not to go? At age forty, it is a real question: What is worth risking one's life for? What is the meaning of risk? At twenty, it sounds like Hamlet—"To be, or not to be."

All of us were experiencing the very same thing, except Margiani, who looked at us with a sly smile, knowing ahead of time what the outcome of our hesitations would be. We went in two ropeteams, working our way across the ridge and chopping every meter of the "knife" with our ice axes. Every second we remembered Shaliko's instructions: If one of the team falls to the left, the other must immediately throw himself to the right—that is the only chance of rescue.

Along the ridge stretched a precipice, the bottom of which we did not see. Luckily for us, the canyon below was like an enormous trough overflowing with thick, soapy foam and swirling, snow-white clouds. That saved us from the feeling of depth and of the irreversibility of a fall into the chasm. Ahead of us the ridge changed to frighteningly steep cliffs that appeared totally impassable. This exit out of the frying pan into the fire brought even greater anxiety. However, the cliffs proved easier than they looked from a distance. Belaying carefully—here is where we no longer considered belaying an idle matter—we overcame them without any particular difficulty. Finally, the jagged, sawlike top led us out onto the highest point of Peak Kavkaz, 4,030 meters.

Shaliko threw aside the stones of the cairn and retrieved a salmon can pierced in several places. The majority of the holes were almost perfect circles, with smooth, unserrated edges, rusted from time. The outline of one of them was cast with the blue of a fresh opal. Shaliko gazed at it, shook his head several seconds, and said, "In the long run everything works out for the better. It's in vain that Russians do not respect the good word 'if.' I like it. If we had found Peak Vulley on time, if we had arrived at Peak Kavkaz a little earlier, it would have been no good."

We understood neither the meaning of these holes nor of Margiani's words.

Leva asked, "Why did they make holes?"

"Because... they were playing around."

"Who?"

"The bolts of lightning."

"And why do you like the word 'if' so much?" Stepanov became interested.

"It's a good word! 'If'—it means: make a mental note of it! Do you know why the lightning struck the can?"

"Metal—power of attraction."

" 'Power!' You also have power. But go try and pull a train car toward yourself. The can only corrected the strike; the summit itself attracted it. That means there is ore in its rock. If that is not chance, then we would not know that one can come here only in good weather. Look at the hole. Fresh. Two to three hours ago it did not exist. If we had come a little earlier, who knows how it would have ended?"

In the can was a note, burned around the edges, from some English climbers, dated 1953. That meant nobody had been here for six years!

We descended in an athletic manner: Shaliko first spent a long time selecting a more reliable ledge. Then, having found a massive stone horn that reminded us of a mooring post, he beat the sharp corners with a hammer so that they would not cut the nylon threads under pressure. He threw on a runner and threaded the rope through it. In turn each of us attached one end of the rope to his belt and wrapped the other end around his arm for greater friction, making it possible to hold himself. Letting out the rope a little at a time, we could then rappel downwards. As we did this we pushed out from the slope with our feet, as if walking. Our instructor did not forget to remind us once more that the descent is the most dangerous part of a climb.

It is not technically dangerous. Rather, the mind destroys the climber. After a climb, the feeling of being prepared and the sharpness of eye decrease, even in an experienced climber. Fatigue, the intoxication of victory and the feeling that the present task is physically easier are all responsible. Statistics say, in fact, that most accidents happen on the descent.

We descended slowly, and Shaliko got angry looking at our steady movements. He was particularly bothered by Stasik, who could not get the rhythm of the movement at all: feed the rope out—descend; feed out—descend. He would either grasp the rope with a death grip, not letting himself down so much as a centimeter, or the opposite, let out so much rope that the momentum of his descent grew dangerous. Then, grasping the nylon rope out of fear, he would take a long time to decide on the next move.

It was quite late when, having gone five full rope-lengths, we found ourselves on a snowy ridge. Here we discovered our old, barely noticeable tracks, and we quickly approached the tents along them. The sky finally cleared, and the head of Elbrus, blue with a greenish tint, stood out sharply against the background of stars and moon.

Sleep overcame me the same second, and so deeply that I awoke at four in the morning feeling I had just closed my eyes. But my head was fresh and clear. I wanted to jump up out of my bag immediately and stretch.

I went out of the tent. But before I had gone more than two steps I flung myself backwards, exactly as if I had run into a lamppost. Right in front of me in a triangular scrap of sky, bound by two neighboring peaks, stood—precisely stood—a huge, distinct shadow of a giant framed by a rosy, shining mount.

The giant repeated my movements and disappeared when I hid in the tent.

Margiani woke up. I showed him the miracle. He laughed and said, "Tsk-tsk, Shatayev! Frightened by your own shadow! That's called the 'Brocken-spectra phenomenon.' In the Hertz massif in Germany there's a small summit, Brocken—1,142 meters. It was there that this phenomenon was noticed for the first time. You see, dense cloud. And a shadow lies on it as on a wall. It will soon be here."

We were ready to leave, only the tents remaining to be rolled up, when suddenly viscous, watery-milky tongues began to engirdle the cliffs around us. The air had the smell of a fresh lake, infused with needles. The cloud filled the hollow of the pass, and I saw the birth of snowflakes. The emptiness became matter, unexpectedly and magically, as if "nothing" was turning into "something." I noticed a dialectical jump— in front of my eyes a philosophical abstraction was being given material form. I had the good fortune to observe one of the secrets of life. It was worth becoming involved in climbing for this alone.

Shaliko and I were together on the same rope coming down from the pass. He praised me generously and several times let me take the lead. I laughed off the compliments modestly, but in my heart I was flattered.

"Some become mountaineers almost on the first climb," he said to me. "Others go and go, and never get beyond the second degree of difficulty. I am talking not to flatter you, but so that you will believe in yourself."

I believed—more than I should have. I felt myself almost an equal with him, although Margiani was a Master of Sports. He walked, as they say, as if at play. His stride was unfettered, exact, and automatic. The technique of breaking trail had obviously long since ceased to be a subject of trouble for him, like walking on toes for a ballerina.

We moved along a slope heavily covered by what must

have been a quite recent snowfall. Now the sun's rays had made the slopes a little like dough. The wet snow stuck to our soles, filling in the tread and destroying precious friction.

Finding myself in front, I tried to walk just as spiritedly as Shaliko. But the steps turned out sloppy, and Margiani, with all his experience, had difficulty correcting them—a slight frost quickly crusted them over.

Fortified by praise, I drifted off into dreams, imagining how I would arrive in Kislovodsk and appear before my friends as a mountaineer. I already saw myself a conqueror of Elbrus. I was proud that I did not talk idly and savored the opportunity to tell them about it. I dreamed of meeting Elvira, a girl I only dreamed about then, and of the admiration in her eyes and the scene where I announced to her, "I know how to get my way. And I will get you." (Later it turned out that my feelings had been reciprocated for a long time, even in the absence of climbing feats.)

While my heart was singing these self-flattering songs, my brain producing these hallucinations of masculine irresistibility, and my own shadow, distorted by the Brockenspectra, seeming like the shadow of a true giant, a bigger and bigger sole of snow was accumulating on my boots and turning to ice. I could see the camp below and observers watching us with binoculars. Shaliko shouted and I looked around. He was pointing at his boots with his ice axe. "He wants to relieve me," I thought. I brushed it aside and headed on.

But I had not gone five steps when my right foot, taking my weight, suddenly slipped sharply downwards. I wanted to hold myself with my left foot, but that only made the situation worse—I spun like a compass, fell on my back, and tumbled head over heels. The slope began to depart somewhere upwards. The rucksack on my back slid like a sled and its weight helped me gain speed. I instinctively tried to grasp the surface with my free hand, which I had balled into a fist.

Shaliko, angered by my insubordination, had decided to quicken his step in order to come alongside and give me a scolding. But first he had stopped to check his own boots, adjust his rucksack, and rub his hands together, so to speak. He noticed me when I was already gaining speed. He immediately thrust his ice axe in with all his might, threw the rope across it, and, lying on the head of the axe with his whole body, waited for the jerk.

By then I was already close to that fatal momentum when self-arrest is almost impossible. I flung my axe several times, trying to brake, but the pick cut freely through the loose snow.

It's difficult to say whether my instinct for self-preservation worked consciously, but suddenly I drew my legs in, threw them toward my head, and, having gone head over heels, felt support under my feet. But the momentum jerked me backwards, threw me on my back, and moved me on. Again I felt the slipping, but now not so fast. I did one more somersault and slowed up enough so that I could get to my feet. I rode on them about two meters, holding myself up with my ice axe...

Having stopped with my face looking upwards, I immediately saw Margiani. He was lying on his axe and waiting for the jerk. But there was none. He looked around, looked at me, and sank back into the snow.

The second team appeared and all three descended to me. I had to look them in the eye, and that was difficult. But Leva and Stasik, frightened and lost, unable to find words, grasped my hand in praise and started to shake it fervently. They did not understand my guilt. They did not understand, although Margiani had explained everything to them on the way. It seemed to them impossible to take such small things into account. Moreover, they thought with conviction, as I had a minute ago, that to record all this jumble of trivial details on behavior and think about them constantly is not only beyond the capacity of the human brain but is also harmful, since it is not climbing but rather constant caution. A novice is convinced that any accident in the mountains is chance, which does not depend on the climber. In his heart he does not believe that the many accident-free years of experienced masters are explained by scrupulous self-control. In order to uderstand that constant caution is also a sign of high-class mountaineering, one has to be a mature mountaineer.

Shaliko stood to one side, his back to me. I could not make up my mind to start talking to him, feeling that words of apology now would sound like the hysterics of one who has experienced a fright, and would make him more angry.

In camp, when his Caucasian anger had quieted down, he came up to me and asked why I had gone on in response to his suggestion to stop and clean our treads with our axes.

"I didn't understand," I answered. "I thought you wanted to relieve me."

"If that's so," he said, "why didn't you obey?"

I was silent.

"Did you feel like a Snow Leopard?* It's my fault. I driveled over a novice. You are all, to the last one, Brocken phenomena. Your own imagination makes you giants."

I had not noticed that Anufrikov had come up to us. From behind I heard a voice:

"He's right in what he's telling you, Volodya. I thought you were a disciplined person. But you . . . Imagine: a person wants to grab a wire, but it's carrying a current. Someone yells at him 'Stop!' And he, you see, is very important and wants to be convinced of things, wants first to be explained the nature of electricity. But not only is there no time to explain, it is not always necessary. Remember: in climbing, every step is a live wire."

It was before dinner. The fellows in the camp, waiting for the bell, were walking around aimlessly in lines. Having noticed Anufrikov, several climbers approached us, anticipating an interesting, lively conversation.

---

*See Chapter 11 — Ed.

"Am I telling the truth, Seryozha?" Mihail Ivanovich asked, turning to a lanky, dark-haired man of the second rating. The question was rhetorical; no answer was expected. But Seryozha himself loved to discuss and generalize, and he did not want simply to assent.

"What are you talking about?"

"I'm telling him that in mountaineering there has to be an acute sense of discipline. He has to have an immediate reaction to a command—even a reflex. He should have, as they say, a reflex discipline. Is that correct or not?"

"I don't think so completely, Mihail Ivanovich."

"How so? Are you against discipline or something?"

"Also not completely. I'm against the idealization of discipline. When I was studying at the institute there was a certain incident. As part of our practical-work requirement our group was sent out logging. We cut wood. Well, we also loaded and transported it, of course. Once it happened that the logs were longer than the truck and trailer allowed. We rolled one pine log up, but it hung down, almost touching the ground. The driver, Volodya Stepanov, did not want to go at first. He resisted awhile, but then agreed. He lengthened the trailer hitch with a thick wire and moved the trailer back. The log lay normally. We loaded it so that there was one meter of empty space between the butts of the logs and the front wall.

"Six sat on the logs. The seventh, the brigade leader, sat next to the driver. Riding on logs, especially on a dirt road through the woods, is no fun—you are shaken and tossed around. And it's frightening—at any moment you could be thrown onto the ground. The student who was sitting closest to the cab didn't resist the temptation—he went and jumped into the deadly space between the wall and the logs. And then the road went downhill... The logs, which were tilted, not braced against anything, and not secured by the rope loop around them, moved from their place with a squeak, at first not quickly but then faster and faster toward the front wall, where this student was standing with his face to the cab, leaning on the roof.

" 'Stop!' we began to yell in terror.

"A driver has a strong reaction to this word and—sufficient discipline. He has a reflex to the word 'stop': his foot instantly presses the brake pedal. Here just that, the brake, was the last straw in speeding up the killer.

"Luckily, for Stepanov this reflex discipline of yours was not important. Instead, his head was in place. To our 'Stop!' he threw his foot from the brake pedal and pressed the accelerator all the way to the floor. The machine darted forward—the logs moved backwards. There's discipline for you, Mihail Ivanovich!"

"Well, so what? No, here is not only a contradiction but also an analogy. An external similarity. The driver knew they were laymen and that they didn't have the right to advise, much less give commands. He didn't pay any attention to your shouts, as a soccer player doesn't pay attention to the yelling of fans. The fact that he had a good reaction and managed to understand that you were ignoramuses and your 'Stop!' was no more than an exclamation is a different conversation. Giving commands and advice can be done only by professionals, and even then only by those who are involved in the situation."

"Okay. Imagine that colleagues of the driver were sitting on the logs. Certainly they too would have yelled 'Stop!' After all, you are right—it is actually no more than an exclamation of horror. It seems funny, but the yell was directed at the logs that were moving toward a person and were about to crush him before our eyes."

"From this you want to make a conclusion: is discipline good always and everywhere? I will answer—always and everywhere. If you doubt this and observe discipline selectively, then you reject it as a method of collective operation for people. If the method is not completely perfect, if it justifies itself ninety percent of the time but not one hundred percent, then it does not follow from this that the method should be crossed off completely. Cross it off because it is not ideal? Sometimes one just has to accept it."

"One doesn't need to cross it off completely," said Sergei. "Partially."

"No, my friend. I repeat: discipline is the kind of concept that, if you doubt it partially, you tear it down completely."

"And I think, Mihail Ivanovich, that radicals are bad, but orthodox people are not honey. I think that if you ask some kind of super-computer what is needed for an ideal life, it will answer: at least one part devil for every nine parts good in a human. In life everything is correct only in part. Look, you're fighting for ideal discipline out of kindness toward people. But I—also out of kindness toward them—want a little lack of discipline, precisely in that one-in-ten situation where your method doesn't work. In the future, humanity will cease to idealize pure concepts, cease to strive toward them. It will reject the opinion that the smarter the better; the more honest the better; the more disciplined the better. People will speak and ask only about proportions. One will assure you, say, that a philosopher needs two parts stupidity for eight parts mind. Another will answer, 'Nothing of the kind! The best combination is six to four.' "

5. The Route to a Bittersweet Dream
(1960)

Those somersaults on the way down from Shkheldinsky Pass set my mountaineering state of mind in the best direction. The school I completed in those few seconds gave me eternal knowledge. During the next session, the praise-stingy Mihail Ivanovich did not tire of mentioning my climbing discipline.

The summer was snowy (it sounds absurd, but it is a fact). Even the slopes that were usually green sparkled with whiteness. Avalanches were frequent in the mountains. Simple routes became difficult, and difficult ones were impossible at times. In areas where, earlier, rests had awaited travelers, one had to break trail.

There was enough work. But evidently the winter training in Moscow and the experience of the previous season, which had solidified during this time, showed themselves. Even on the summit sections of routes, I did not particularly overstrain myself. I climbed them confidently enough, feeling a reserve of endurance. In short, I did not have to experience that unbearable fatigue that makes even a favorite activity dismal and torturing.

I was named leader for West Irikchat (1b degree of difficulty). It was because of this that some unpleasantries, which I had expected least of all, started.

After my appointment Kostya Smirnov behaved as though I had taken his favorite girl away. On the route he was ideally obedient, but he did not take his critical eyes off me, noting my every slip. At rests he did not miss a chance to mention them in a subtle way. I sensed his look and felt fettered. It seemed to me that I made more mistakes than I should have.

In his heart he justifiably felt that he was not inferior to me in either physical or moral strength. Most of all, he was genuinely convinced of the opposite. Indeed, he had excellent mountaineering qualities—he knew that well. But as a conceited person, he made superficial judgments about people and saw them in a light that reflected favorably on himself. He took my unwillingness to argue with him as intellectual weakness. But it was boring for me to engage in the casuistic battles to which Kostya was particularly inclined.

He was voluble, energetic, and given to controversy. He willingly undertook proving that a mouse is stronger than an elephant and that it is better to be a rabbit than a boa constrictor. He would get the last word, thinking he had gained a victory, and afterwards, in his heart, he would despise his opponent and be delighted with himself.

In our relationship he felt himself the leader, certain that he was smarter and stronger. Therefore he took my appointment as an insulting injustice.

The climb went successfully. In the process, moreover, I fulfilled the requirements for the third rating and thereby descended a rated person. But my happiness was not complete—my time at the camp was coming to an end, and I still had not been on Elbrus.

As in the previous year, a group of fellows including Uspensky, Smirnov, and myself decided to obtain a second period at the camp, this time for ten days. Anufrikov undertook to petition Tenishev, the head of the camp. He did not dare refuse "the father," as they called Mihail Ivanovich, openly, but he made two stipulations. First, the passes would cost the full twenty-day price.

"Second," he said, "Do they want to stay? Okay, but they must repeat the training on cliffs, ice, and scree again."

"Why?" asked the dumbfounded Anufrikov. "That was all covered only twenty days ago."

"Because they are mastering the science of mountaineering too hurriedly. Your Shatayev received a badge in a year, and then he got the third rating right away in his second year."

"So what? Is that bad? Why the ill feeling?"

Tenishev turned away toward the window and looked out, as if the answer might be found there. The instructor Bushin, who had been sitting silently until now, answered instead. Suddenly jumping up, he started to jabber in a contradictory and incoherent fashion:

" 'Bad,' 'ill feeling'—boy, the ones who ripen quickly are breeding. They want to become masters immediately! I've been working on the second rating for six years, and look— he came, he saw, he conquered!"

"Oh, that's what it is! 'A friend's success is a stain on my uniform.' I understand."

Luckily for us, Zak, the supervisor of the alpine region, was in camp at that moment. When Anufrikov told him about Tenishev's stipulations he also asked, "What for?"

"Go and ask him," answered "the father." "He's afraid of youth. He fears its growth."

"Let them select a route and go as they please. Concerning the passes—talk to the division. The passes can be divided. After all, there's no reason for them to hang around here for the whole twenty days. One pass can be split between two climbers."

The All-Union Division—Abalakov, Arkin, Budanov, and Anufrikov—decided to give us divided passes. Nonetheless, the head of the camp added a resolution to my application: "to pay the cost of a stay in camp for twenty days."

Mihail Ivanovich decided to do something about this "robbery," but I prevailed on him to leave things as they were.

My hardships did not end here, however. Somewhere on the last section of the West Irikchat traverse, right before descending to camp, Kostya Smirnov had finally changed his anger into kindness and regarded me cordially. Below, when we were sorting things out, he had not directed one bad word toward me. And during the two to three days while the question of the passes was decided, the previous friendly warmth continued in our relations. But as soon as it became known that we were to stay, he resumed his egotistical behavior. He tried to persuade everyone that there was no need at all to include me in the group, discussing this with each person separately, *tête-à-tête*. Shatayev, he said, will only hinder us since "having been corrupted" into an experienced leader, he will get his hands into everything and take over. Then he talked about it openly, in the tent where the whole group gathered. They disagreed with him in a friendly way. Uspensky proposed that I lead again. It turned out that the fellows had already talked about this with "the father," and he had agreed.

When our discussion concluded, Kostya disappeared somewhere and he was gone for an hour and a half. Soon, Anufrikov appeared in the tent, looking sullen, even morose.

"Well, there you are," he said, "the celebrated collective! Abalakov and Budanov think that you should be cited for 'high collectivism and harmony of action in difficult weather conditions.' However, not everything is as good with you as it seems. Smirnov was just at my tent. He flatly refused to go under Shatayev's leadership. Out of principle. He thinks special conditions are being made for Shatayev. I'm not asking for your opinion. There's no time for discussion—I know that this is Smirnov's personal opinion. However, one also has to consider personal opinions, since there must be peace and agreement on a climb—between everyone. I was forced to find a leader elsewhere. Instructor Misha Hergiani has agreed."

An hour later Hergiani approached us to say that Tenishev would not allow the group out given its present makeup. Since most members of the group were badge carriers [novices], it did not have the right to go without an instructor. And since Misha was going as the leader, we still needed an instructor.

"There's a petty bureaucrat for you indeed." The "father" fell into a fit of temper and undertook to find an instructor. But for some reason they were all tied up with urgent business.

Two of the ten days were thus spent idly. The third, it appeared, would not pass any better.

"It seems we should gather our junk and go to the station," Chistoforov said to me. "If the authorities don't want something, then the matter is finished!"

" 'Father' will think of something."

"What *is* he for you, the Lord God?"

Anufrikov turned out to be, if not the Lord God, at least nothing less than King Solomon. He found the ideal solution. He went to the rescue leader and, as if by chance, asked, "What's it like in the mountains now? What are the snow conditions?"

The other immediately understood what was being said because, like most people in the camp, he was aware of our problem. An entertaining scene was played out. They were... both choking with laughter. Having fixed their gaze at each other, barely opening their mouths so as not to burst out laughing, they said through their teeth:

"You ask how's the snow? Well, who knows? After all, I myself have not seen it."

"That's bad. After all, you're the rescue leader—you should know!"

"That's bad. I'm the rescue leader, it's delegated to me."

"You should go, find out. Maybe there's no snow at all?"

"I should go. Only there's nobody to go with. No groups have gone out for quite a few days. The instructors are busy—they're writing instructions in a hundred copies. Am I to go alone into the mountains?"

"That's bad." The "father" shook his head.

"That's bad." The rescue leader shook his head.

"Shatayev, ask the fellows whether they need to go into the mountains.... But do you have an instructor's certificate?"

"Yes. Only it's threadbare.'

"Why?"

"I've taken it to Tenishev to be checked."

"Often?"

"Not really. Three times—at breakfast, lunch, and dinner."

We finally went to bed calmly, sure about the next day—for the first time in the last few days.

In the morning we fell into lineup, impatiently awaiting the order to set off—but there was no order. Tenishev demanded that the route committee give their approval. At that time such formalities still existed. In practice, however, the checking of equipment and the knowledge of the route was taken care of by one of the leaders, by the "permission-giver." This had been the case for many years in the climbing camps. Shortly thereafter the practice was made official.

Of all the spikes that the camp head had put in our wheels, this was the most open. Obviously, nobody knew who was on the committee. One of the climbers, helping us in our search, suddenly discovered that he himself was among its members.

When the equipment check was finished a new instruction came from Tenishev: our departure could be allowed only after the orders had been written. This demand arrived, again, during lineup. Budanov approached Tenishev with such a look that Anufrikov threw himself between them, just in case. But the former merely filtered through his teeth, syllable by syllable, "We'll write the orders afterwards!"

Tenishev wanted to answer but could not make up his mind what to say.

Elbrus was later. First Dzhantugan. The ascent of this peak took us only one day.

Dzhantugan was my first classic route—vertical walls, difficult ice overgrown with seracs, and sharp snow ridges along the top of which one had to go. This summit is classified as 3a degree of difficulty.

We took Anatoly Kustovsky's note, which was dated August 1959, and in thirty minutes were down, going on our rear ends here and there.

And now, at last...

They took us by car up to the village of Terskol, and from there, on June 28, my climb to the summit of Elbrus began.

Elbrus, stretching out like a gray serpentine of a road spiraling up for three thousand meters, was quiet and still. Only here, below, was there a slight southwest breeze. It made its way under our rucksacks and covered our necks, which were protected by our caps, with a pleasant freshness.

We were on our way to Hut Eleven. We walked quickly, as if afraid the camp authorities would chase us. The farther we went from camp, the calmer we became in our hearts and the more we believed that finally we were on our way to Elbrus.

Before reaching the base of the ice—at checkpoint 150— we stopped for about ten minutes to rest. There we met a group of hikers who had rested and spent the night there. Their "summit"—the highest point toward which they were striving—was Hut Eleven. They looked at us with respect, taking us for veteran climbers who, moreover, were going to Hut Eleven in a single spurt! How were they to know that we had barely reached the third rating? Of course, we did not begin to disappoint them—it is very pleasant to bask in the admiration of others. We were novices and still susceptible to such worship. But in secret this unearned recognition jarred our hearts.

At Hut Eleven, ignoring the fact that Misha Hergiani could not find the route list in his pockets (he had left it in camp), without which the head of the hut, Kudinov, did not have the right to let us go on; and ignoring the troubles that befell Kudinov—he was forced to call the camp by radio—everything went smoothly.

We did not waste time. While they were clarifying the legality of our group we went out to begin acclimating ourselves ·[to the altitude and weather].

One and a half hours of unhurried ascent and we were at the Pastuhov Cliffs. There were traces of a temporary military encampment there—growing up through the snow were broken stands and meteorological apparatuses with gauges. They were peeling and eaten by corrosion and rust. One often comes across such traces in the Caucasus. They say that in the transparent depths of the glacier, as if in a glass-enclosed museum case, the results of the mountain campaign of the Edelweis division—corpses of the Fascists—were "displayed" for a long time. Misha said that you used to be able to see this "open" cemetery until quite recently, but that a couple of years ago it was destroyed by explosions....

It was a difficult trip: The altitude had already made itself felt (dizziness, nausea) and as if out of spite, the weather deteriorated. As the temperature dropped and the wind grew stronger, we hid behind rocks; and although subjecting ourselves to this severe cold was nearly intolerable, we stayed there for two hours in order to get better acclimated.

Upon descending and entering the living area of the hut, we were struck by the civilized comforts of these mere earthlings—folding beds, chintz curtains on the windows, rice soup with dill. This mood made it necessary for us first to sit at the table with the domino players before heading for the club to dance with the hikers, who were even happier than we were because they had now reached their Chomolungma—Hut Eleven.

The next day, following our own tracks, we took a second conditioning trip. This time we went about three hundred meters higher. I passed the previous day's extreme limit without noticing, not believing that just the day before, this altitude made me want to quickly descend. At the Pastuhov Cliffs only Kolya Smolensky complained of pain in his head and stomach. The crisis will pass, we thought. But the farther we went, the worse it became.

Hergiani decided he had to go down and ordered me to accompany him. Too bad! I wanted to go farther, but there was nothing to do. We attached ourselves to the polyethylene line and descended quickly to the hut.

One o'clock in the morning. I put on three pairs of wool socks, two sweaters, and two pairs of pants. The parka fit tightly over it all, but it did fit. My boots were greased, the tread in good shape. Everything checked out. I could go.

Beyond the wall of the hut, the temperature was 15°C below zero. What was it there, on top? The night was black. Only in the south were the stronger stars breaking through the shroud of clouds. We walked in three groups of two. Uspensky and I were a team. The cold was affecting us—it encouraged us, pushed us toward a good pace. Only Kolya Smolensky dragged along at the rear, continually sticking his hands in his pockets, hurriedly chewing prunes. He was a strong-willed person, but obviously altitude was not for him.

Hergiani took him on himself—they were one team. I walked and thought, "Misha is a good fellow!" Someone else would have left him in the hut, and that would have been the end of it. Misha preferred going last, tying himself, as is said, hand and foot, but not depriving a friend of hope.

Uspensky and I were walking in front, trying as best we could in the dark to find our tracks from the day before. It was useless—could they have melted?

The Route to a Bittersweet Dream (1960)

Toward three o'clock, as it was getting light, we finally noticed twenty-five meters to the left a dotted furrow, covered slightly with fresh snow. But there was no sense in deviating now—we were at the Pastuhov Cliffs.

Before leaving the hut Hergiani warned us, "Follow strictly in twos!" Then, after a hundred meters, he stopped and said again, "Follow strictly in twos!" He was speaking to everyone, but looking at Smirnov.

The Pastuhov Cliffs are a traditional rest spot. But we could not last longer than five minutes—our toes would freeze with inactivity. Once again Misha said, "Follow strictly in twos!" We kept going.

Uspensky and I were in front, as before. The snow squeaked under our feet, as if in song. There was resilience and vigor in everything: in the air, in the snow, in my own body. The steps turned out well and were easy to make.

I had stopped to adjust the straps of my rucksack when Uspensky shouted out to me. Smiling, he nodded back over his shoulder, telling me to look. Kostya Smirnov and Valery Chistoforov, the pair walking behind us, were separated. Smirnov was hurriedly approaching us. In several meters his heavy breathing was audible, but there was a happy smile on his face: finally, he says, I caught up.

"Did something happen?" Leva asked.

"Nothing. Finally I caught up to you."

"But the order was to go in twos!"

Kostya did not catch this and moved ahead silently.

A shout came from below. Hergiani waved his hands, threatening with his fist.

"It seems that Misha is demanding that you wait for Chistoforov," Uspensky said to Smirnov.

"I'm not in the army. There are a lot of such sergeants—why should I drag along if I can go quickly?"

Hergiani was making it clear with gestures that one of us should descend. It was more than three hundred meters down to him. Smirnov walked without looking around. I wanted to catch up to him and stick his face in the snow, to cool that ambitious heat. Leva guessed what I was thinking and looked hopefully at me, as if to say, Let's teach this person once and for all. But I came to my senses—fights have no place on climbs. I had to head down.

Hergiani, showing his indignation toward Kostya, started to yell at me in a fit of temper.

"If that upstart doesn't calm down," he shouted "I'll turn the whole group back!"

Up again. With difficulty I caught up—the two of them were walking like circus horses in a riding school.

Kostya, his face distorted with anger, heard my announcement out. Casting a fierce glance at me, he bit his lip, and without saying a word waited for the others.

Leva and I were permitted to move up to the saddle itself. But my having had to hike down and back up, and almost at a run, was not without consequences. Approaching the col, I suddenly felt nauseous, my vision darkened, the slope spun around. I managed to drive my ice axe in and literally fell on it with my chest. I closed my eyes. Was this the point? Was five thousand meters really my limit? Was I a climber for whom even the Caucasian heights are too much? Would my dreams collapse altogether on my first attempt? There it was, my athletic limit—and life limit too. My destiny was to putter around below—to get up by the alarm clock, to leave home by the bell, to read *Soviet Sports,* to argue with passengers on the trams about the merits of a soccer team, to watch television in the evening, to go to the movies on Saturdays, and on payday to look for drinking buddies. At such times there is self-examination: thus I knew then exactly what I was capable of.

No! My self-examination was only beginning!

I bemoaned my fate for several seconds, while deep in my heart I knew that now I would straighten up and go on. I would move upwards, stopping only if I lost consciousness.

Having waited until I felt better, I pulled my ice axe out and took three slow steps. But again I felt nausea, again the mountains began to play tricks. Another stop, rest, and so for fifty meters. All this time Leva Uspensky did not move a step away from me.

The second team caught up to us. Smirnov unexpectedly showed some concern; he said something kind and friendly. He would not go any farther without me, and he gave his word about it, ardently and decidedly. But his persuasions were superfluous, if only because by this time I was feeling much better.

Finally, we reached the col. From below it had seemed as though you could sit in it and dangle your feet in different directions, as on the back of a two-humped camel. But it turned out that you could put a train across it and still maneuver the train. From below it had seemed that by jumping agilely from the col, you could grasp the upper edge of the east tower. But it turned out that the difference in size between an ant and a camel's hump was probably less—except that an ant goes a thousand times faster and more easily on a camel's hump than we did on the east tower of Elbrus. Even so, you only had to look down for it to become immediately clear: this was nothing compared to what we had already done. No, the troubles of an ant cannot be compared to the troubles of people.

We threw our rucksacks down and sat to wait for Hergiani and Smolensky. They soon approached, but Kolya looked bad. His eyes were huge, unblinking, incapable of smiling, his cheeks drooping... not much was left. I wanted to believe he could make it. It was the second day this fellow was breaking himself with courage. There was no shame for any of us in bowing before it.

One last obstacle—the east tower—lay between us and our goal. We traversed its slope, skirting to the left, when around a bend we suddenly saw the hut! It looked foreign, covered with felt, packed with snow here and there under the roof, and engraved in the usual monotone, but unexpectedly fairytale-like. For some reason it was frightening to peek inside.

There was something mystical in it, although even the Evil One would have been uncomfortable there.

I had heard about this hut below. And not just once. It was surrounded by legend even more than by snow—fellow mountaineers are very skilled craftsmen in this regard. They say that several years ago a group experienced a strange attack here. During the night someone strained at the door, which was blocked with ice axes, and hammered at it with his fists. Then he went up on the roof, tried to break through it, and in a rage filled the mountains with an inhuman roar. In the morning, when everybody had calmed down, they saw tracks of bare feet leading upwards. Some say that they saw the distant figure of a human. Still others go further and erect a halo on his head. All are skeptical about such tales but agree that something *was* there, something with evil intentions! As a rule, such talk leads to discussions about "snowmen" in general.

We squeezed through a small window. All the mysticism instantly disappeared: Lying around on the floor were ropes, a stove, bottles, flare packages. Smolensky and Hergiani arrived about twenty minutes later. We began to believe that Kolya was still capable of continuing the assault. His eyes were livelier. His face, though exhausted, was rid of the gray-green look of anemia, which had become to seem normal with him. I thought that not one of us deserved the victory as much as he did.

Misha Hergiani decided to increase Kolya's chances. We had to set out quickly, but he gave Smolensky a half-hour rest. Who would stay with him?

"Either Shatayev or Smirnov," Hergiani said. "But Shatayev helped him descend yesterday. That means Smirnov should stay."

The firn, smooth and as dense as hard rock, sparkled in the sun, which was at an angle almost parallel to the slope. The points went in with difficulty, such that the tracks were almost invisible. It was incomprehensible how one managed to penetrate this glazed hardness with them at all.

The summit was getting closer. The fulfillment of my dream was getting closer. And the closer it got, the faster, the more impatiently I moved toward it. The last fifty meters. Leva lagged behind just a little, but there was no holding me back. And finally, there it was! Before me was the huge cone of the crater sloping down, like an amphitheater. To the right, along its edge, about two hundred meters, was a bright, easily noticeable pedestal—the summit cairn.

For the time being I did not touch the note—I was waiting for Leva. I urged him on, I shouted to go faster, but he shook his head—he could not go faster. Then, suddenly, a figure appeared from behind the bend that Uspensky had just passed. He was going quickly, resiliently, and evenly, not slowing his pace on the increased steepness, actually engaging a supplementary "engine." I saw that it was not Hergiani, nor Chistoforov, although one would have expected them by now. I could not see his features at such a distance, but I recognized him by his walk, by his manner of moving.

Smirnov overtook Leva quickly and approached me. He was alone. He came up and embraced me. But I chilled his ardor with the question, "Where's Kolya? With Hergiani?"

"No. He stayed in the hut. I didn't insist—he wouldn't have made it anyway."

"You didn't insist... You insisted on the opposite!"

"He wouldn't have made it anyway."

"Did you tell him that?"

We all gathered at the cairn, but our joy was marred, as if we had been stung by a wasp. Fate very rarely presents us with even a second of ideal happiness, and the flavor of the Elbrus trip was contaminated by bitterness. Even so, I reached my goal; I kept my word.

6. Strange Mountains
(1957–1963)

I was timid before her. She had a daring look, a sharp tongue, and a head full of mischievous fantasies. She could not stand insincerity. She saw through it like a clairvoyant and with a youthful directness destroyed it with taunts and ridicule. Her nature was romantic. She valued chivalry in a man and in the depths of her heart regretted that women could not show this quality.

She was always in the center of a group, regardless of where or how intellectual it was. Artists, scientists, and writers who populated the climbing couloirs, who at one time were her fellow classmates, and who later were her colleagues in industry: they all—honestly speaking—pampered her with attention. A person so thrust into the limelight and subject to the scrutiny of others cannot gain the "mark" of authority merely from having read more than a hundred books or from having even the most prestigious profession. Rather, authority is proportional to a person's independence and to self-sufficiency. Elvira was independent in her thoughts, actions, judgments, and views, which probably made her attractive. She had her own voice, and that made her a leader. Only later did I find that with all this she was far from always being sure of herself, painfully experiencing each of her blunders, and was easily wounded.

But that was later. At first we had a superficial, purely professional acquaintance. Then I dared only to think about her—I did not have enough nerve to take the initiative. After several years had passed she told me I underrated myself often and in many things, and therefore received many pleasant surprises from life. I do not know whether it is so or not, but she herself seemed to me precisely such a happy surprise.

Our formal acquaintance broke off—she changed jobs. We did not see each other for more than two years. But suddenly, (it sounds too much like a cheap detective story to seem trustworthy, but it is true all the same) one evening, upon returning home after a hard day, I sat down to eat supper, having decided that afterwards I would go to bed immediately. My mother came up to me and, squinting at a piece of paper, said, "Some girl called you."

"What girl?" I asked sluggishly, pretending that it did not interest me very much. Nothing intrigues people of that age more than an unexpected call from a girl. I was no exception.

"Her name was Elya. She left her number. I relied on my memory, thinking, I'll hang up and write it down. But by the time I found paper and pencil, I had forgotten half of it. Something like this. Look."

I dialed the number right away. They did not know any Elya there. Mother had mixed up some numbers. If only I knew which.

All the following evening I turned the dial, changing the number combinations. The next evening the same. Then the third. And so on for five days, until my fingers were swollen. During that time I spoke with many Elviras, even with Elvira Sergeyevna. But none of them was the right one.

And then, without any hope, only to try one more variation, I dialed the next number and said the full first name, patronymic, and surname. In the receiver I heard a sarcastic "Hmm," and then, "Elya, some official is calling." Then her voice came on the line.

"Hello, Elya. This is Volodya Shatayev."

At first silence, then, "I had already decided that you wouldn't call."

"Sorry. I was figuring out your number."

"How did you figure it out?"

"Process of elimination."

"For four days?"

"Five."

She laughed. Then she asked, "Well, how are you?"

"It's not worth talking on the phone. It would be better if we got together," I dared. "Then I could see you."

"Well . . . tomorrow."

"No, it's a long time until tomorrow. Better today."

Her objection was weak, and I said, "Fifteen minutes to get ready. At eight o'clock at the Sportivnaya subway station. It's already been five days."

"Not five days, but two years," she answered sharply and hung up the receiver.

She came. In a modest black dress. The blue-eyed girl of Debussy, "with hair the color of straw." Her look was not at all daring—it was trusting.

I remember that at that time I was envious of fellows who could deftly and unpretentiously "go with" girls. A five-kilometer distance was much easier for me. But now I was talking a lot, nonstop, not afraid of stupidities, since she liked everything, no matter what I said. We had a good time, everything seemed funny, and we laughed about everything that we had seen and remembered—not maliciously, but in idle laughter. Suddenly she asked:

"Would you be capable of not going to your mountains?"

That had not occurred to me! I recalled married fellow climbers, dark and morose before leaving for the climbing camps—the annual time of family trouble. On the road—on

Strange Mountains (1957–1963)

the train or in the plane—they would curse, unable to hold back anymore, complaining about limited, selfish wives who were unable and unwilling to understand their passions. They would begin heatedly, and later, having had their say and cooled off their boiling interiors, would end calmly: If you look into it, they would say, they are right—God forbid I should be in their place! And so it would go every time without exception.

"You were startled," she said, "as though I wanted to push you into a bottomless pit. But after all, I simply asked, without any ulterior motives, whether you could or not? Okay, you don't have to answer. I understand everything. Now you'll strain and say 'I can!' And then later you'll go all the same."

"You're right, it seems."

And then I heard still another question: "And can I go with you into the mountains? After all, I'm an athlete, the second rank in skating and bicycling."

The whole winter of 1962 I coached her at our climbing-training camp in Tsaritsyno. Toward the end, she climbed rather freely on the walls of Tsaritsyno Palace. She learned to handle a rope and carabiners satisfactorily. Then came her mountaineering debut in the Caucasus. As a result of it, up to the very spring of 1963 she cursed climbing day in and day out. She cursed the Caucasus and especially the rucksack. In addition, she had been impertinent to the leader of the group, and the latter gave her a poor reference. After all this, Elvira decided she would never go higher than the Lenin Hills in Moscow, and then only if her load did not exceed the weight of a woman's purse.

I was calm about this—it is but one variation of the classical first step in becoming infected with the mountains. In the spring she began fussing and often announced, inopportunely, that she was not going to the mountains, even when I had not asked her about it at all. I pretended to be persuading her. Then she would answer, "I don't know, probably not."

When with the approach of the season some very painstaking doctor found she had a heart problem and forbade her to climb, she cried on my chest. I did not know how to calm her. Then it turned out that the diagnosis was not true.

Her road to climbing began in 1962. Ten years later Master of Sports Elvira Shatayeva and her friends Galina Rozhalskaya, Ilsiar Muhamedova, and Antonina Son were awarded medals "for outstanding athletic achievement in the USSR" for the world's first women's climb of a seven-thousander (Peak Eugenia Korzhenevskaya).

In February 1963 Elvira became Shatayeva [Mrs. Shatayev]. Several months later she was informed that she was a widow ...

o

Where did they appear from, those mountain birds, similar to hens? The snow cocks, clinging to the edges of cliffs, shouted tensely and hysterically, as if amidst a bird slaughter. They were constantly taking off in a fuss, flying about in a panic, landing for a moment, then rushing upward again, unable to find a spot for themselves. Where did those senselessly screaming jackdaw-clouds appear from? I had never seen so many birds at once in the mountains.

The mountains were strange that day—unusually noisy and booming. Avalanches occurred with the frequency of passing cars on an intercity highway. Rocks fell continuously—en mass and one at a time.

There had been nothing like it on our way up. We had been calm even in our hearts, although toward the summit the route had taken us over 5b class of difficulty.

In the Caucasus, there is no exhausting altitude. Instead, in order to reach 5b, we had ascended a route stuffed with unimaginable rock-climbing difficulties. The vertical Dombai-Ulgen, where we were, is a little more than four thousand meters. But in getting to the summit you leave half of yourself on the overhanging cliffs, the rocks, the chimneys, the glass-smooth ledges, and the slabs.

Strange Mountains (1957–1963)

Now, thank God, the leader of the group, Sasha Balashov, had the note he removed in his hand, and our note was on the summit. We were on the descent, about three hundred meters from the highest point. We had an excellent bivouac—the tent was in a cliffy niche. It would seem that we had everything necessary for a serene rest. But there was a restlessness in our hearts from all this incomprehensible, unusual commotion. We did not admit this to one another: there was no visible reason for anxiety. The niche was hidden from avalanches; one would not expect rocks here. What else could it be? Would the mountains themselves come crashing down?

While I was thinking this, a cobblestone, similar in form and size to a calf's liver, pierced the tent and fell at our feet. Balashov suddenly woke up, examined us with a crazed look, and said, "I was just flying!"

Boris Matveyevich Utkin, the oldest in age, answered, "That happens with infants."

"No, not like that," Balashov assured us, not having understood the joke and not having woken up fully. "Something pushed me and tossed me about."

At seven in the evening, when the summer sun is usually still above the horizon, the sky suddenly was completely covered and it became dark. The mountains quieted and lightning cut straight through the twilight, like a spear. It became evident that what was happening in the mountains was nothing more than an overture to a storm. We did not know then that the storm was itself only a piece of the overture.

The lightning energetically and unceasingly broke the alarming, rumbling darkness far and wide. I counted from the flash to the thunder: one, two, three. I multiplied by three hundred [meters] and determined the distance of the thunderclap. Sometimes the sound almost coincided with the flash, which meant it was close by, less than three hundred meters away.

The storm lasted about an hour. Then it quieted and we went to sleep.

Early in the morning I got out of the tent. What a surprise: unprecedented warmth! The air was as fresh as in spring. The snow sheets on the slopes were flowing like streams. Below were the gray tongues of avalanches. The couloirs, the avalanche tracks—everything was in motion, pressing, bustling, like some urgent migration.

From somewhere above, from behind the cliffs, came shouts, discussions. The neighboring groups are already moving, and we've just gotten up, I thought.

Utkin came out of the tent, looked around, and said, "Foehn! A warm front. It must have come from the sea. We need to go down immediately."

We packed our things right away and continued the descent. We went quickly, in three hours covering about a thousand vertical meters. After resting several minutes we were about to move on when a red flare shot up from behind a cloud a little to the right of where the bivouac had been. After it came a second one. A distress signal!

As if on purpose, at that moment below us a band of clouds appeared that was thick enough to completely cover the meadow. It hid the red flares from the sight of observers in camp. Most likely we were the only witnesses to the signal. A new consideration stopped our first rush: to quickly go help. Even more important was to inform the camp, since truly effective help could come only from there. However, we should not run en masse. We were four, and therefore it was simple to decide: two up and two down. We drew lots: Utkin and I would descend to the meadow.

"It's fair," Kolya Rodimov said. "The youngest and the oldest."

We left another thirty meters of steep slope behind us and suddenly—we looked in dismay to the sides. We did not recognize the route! What had happened? Where had we come to?

I remembered well—here, above the wall, razor-sharp cliff ridges stuck up. We were forced to break them with hammers so that they would not cut the ropes under weight. Where did they go? They hadn't been planed off so soon, had they? Was that the wall—monolithic, smooth, so hard that after every hammered piton you are pumped, as they say? Now it was licked clean, like clay—hard, but still damp on the surface, as if it had been plastered. Why would we have driven a piton here if it is all banded with crevices and rocks? But back then there were no crevices or rocks, and the pitons—here they were.

I lay down and stretched out and grabbed the closest one; it remained in my hand. What had happened?

There was no time to figure it out. I pounded in an ice screw, clipped the rope in and, with a belay from Utkin, traversed the wall for about forty meters. Along the way I thrust the pick of my ice hammer into the clay, as into ice. I put weight on it, actually just a little—only to maintain my balance. It held! Such a thing had never happened, at least to me.

At the end of the wall was a shelf, small but spacious enough to settle myself and take a partner. I brought Boris Matveyevich here. In his eyes—no, it was not suspicion or restlessness, it was amazement. The old experienced climber, capable of explaining any trick of the mountains, just spread his hands in helplessness.

The glacier below us now seemed like the Promised Land. There one could breathe freely—though not direct, the road still led toward home. From the shelf where we stood to the desired destination was a drop of not more than a rope's length. Below were overhanging cliffs, and the descent was relatively simple—the usual movement downward along the rope. It demanded not so much dexterity as strength.

The knob we had selected as an anchor was about half a meter from the edge of the platform and resembled a tapering block about forty centimeters across—a monolithic outgrowth of the cliff itself. No anchor could be more reliable! I made a loop in a rappel line and, having thrown the sling over the block, fastened a carabiner to it. All that was left was to flick the rope. No! Until now I had not been fated to suffer from my own negligence; the psychology of belaying was working impeccably and at the proper time. Out of the habit of testing any buttress to which I trusted my life, I kicked the knob... and it broke off.

Before the descent I had wanted to take my rucksack off and attach it to the rope separately. But I had thought: This is a fated hour; anything at all can be expected from these enraged mountains, even more with me. Boris Matveyevich held me.

The glacier. A deep sigh. It looked as if the danger were over. Now for home. We'd get out of here somehow.

Below, on the moraine, Volodya Kavunenko's group was observing us through binoculars. I could see them quite well without glasses: there was Kavunenko, next to him Volodya Verbovoy. Friends were nearby, standing guard, which meant we could rest easy.

When the tension lessened, the rucksack became heavy and made itself felt. In particular, it cut more sharply into the shoulders, and my back burned and itched as if from bedsores. I thought again: Should I take the pack off, if only for a few minutes, while Utkin descends? But I did not—like a passenger who has stood the whole way and does not sit in a vacated seat because he has only one more stop.

Rocks were falling continuously, small ones and huge ones. The huge "suitcases" turned smoothly in the air, fell swiftly, hissing and buzzing, and upon hitting the slope sprayed into small parts as from an explosion. I was in a safe place several meters from the foot of the overhanging wall. Anything that came down the slope from above fell ten steps below me. The flight trajectory of stones deviated from the pure vertical by another ten meters. But you could see the flight, you could see the moment of landing. You knew what would happen every time, and still, instinctively, you huddled and quivered, as if recoiling from a shout.

This bombardment was nothing at all for Utkin, who was

on the wall itself. While he was preparing to descend, I reclined on the ice, resting on my rucksack.

The air, saturated with a bathhouse dampness, was as gray as bare ice ground by the force of water. Steam was pouring out of the bergschrund under the wall about five meters from me. Sometimes the rockfall quieted for a minute, the mountains became peaceful, and I was drawn toward sleep by the motionlessness that had set in.

There was no kind of premonition, no kind of voice of intuition, no internal force pushing. Utkin had already started the descent and was approaching the middle of the rope. A din, a crash, a gnashing split the air, as if worlds were colliding. The mountains swayed. I jumped and, looking upward, saw...

About five hundred meters above me, slowly, indeed with stony impassiveness, the cliff was breaking off. A mass fifty steps across and as many high, having paused on the ridge, held back momentarily, as if deciding where to go—to remain in space or to tumble downward? Then, having crossed this point, it fell toward me with great acceleration.

Amazing! Even now I remember my every move, although at that moment I did not even remember myself. What happened in my head? What battle of the forces of fear, will, and self-preservation?

Five meters from me was the bergschrund, the gap between the glacier and the cliff, where the ice, warmed by the heat of the rock, melts to form a crevasse. The depth of a bergschrund can vary greatly. Sometimes it goes almost to the bottom of the glacier.

I did not know anything about the depth of this bergschrund, for in descending onto the ice I had exhausted my curiosity. I had noticed the bergschrund solely out of the climber's habit of taking note of the topography. Toward the end of a climb all the mountain wonders become boring, so much so that they attract no more attention than the furniture in one's own apartment.

I should have made certain it was not deep. First, a strong

bedding of ice was hardly possible at this lower altitude. Second, the wall was overhanging and faced northwest and therefore was not warmed as much—the sun was not here for long.

But this is the wisdom of hindsight. At the time I was barely thinking at all. I had two choices: to turn my back to the deathly cliff or to jump into the crevasse, in which case I had a small chance of rescue.

Was it terrible to decide on this jump? There was no time to worry. As if on wings I overcame the five steps separating us and jumped down.

Having flown a few meters, I suddenly felt a sharp braking, as though someone above had grabbed hold of my rucksack and was trying to hold on to it. The walls of the bergschrund, as on an express elevator, slowed their fatal race immediately and came to a complete stop. I felt a strong jerk and a sharp pain in my shoulders. The pack straps cut into my body and crackled threateningly.

It was easy to explain it all: the trench, which was a little wider than a meter at the surface, narrowed greatly toward the bottom. My body still could pass through, but the rucksack—one and a half times wider than my shoulders—began to drag in the narrowed crevasse until finally it jammed.

The stop was timely. Under my feet the bergschrund narrowed so much that it would have been difficult to fit my two feet into it. Another half meter and I would have broken my legs, torn them up on the filelike surface of the walls, and finally been jammed so tight that later they would not have been able to pull me out.

At that moment, somewhere on the surface, there was a thunderous rumble. A roaring echo passed along the bergschrund, and an avalanche of rocks rained down on me.

And again my rucksack saved me. Tucking my head against my chest and covering it with my arms, I waited several minutes for that single rock earmarked for me, which, in spite of Newton's law, would follow a particularly complicated trajectory, pass around the rucksack, and come down on my head.

Silence came. But I was afraid to open my eyes and take a breath, although I understood that the danger had passed.

It was even darker than before in the bergschrund and smelled disgustingly of sulphur. Tens of rock corks were jammed in the crevasse—at different levels and of different sizes. In front of me, several centimeters from my face, was an obstruction of crushed rock mixed with ice mush. The ice wall, pitted and warped by the bombardment, abounded in holes and ledges. Now there was something to step on with my feet, something to grasp with my hands.

It was seven or eight meters to the surface. The rucksack did not allow me to be rescued. It was crammed into the crevasse, covered with rock, and unable to budge from its place. Did I really have to destroy it now?

I had gotten my knife out of my pocket and begun to cut through the straps when I heard above me, "Volodya, Volodya! Shatayev!" It was Utkin shouting. I called back.

"Are you alive?"

"Everything's okay."

"Great! Can you attach yourself to the rope?"

"Toss it down."

Boris Matveyevich, in a sweat and worn out, suddenly lost his head, embraced me, patted me on the back, and could not say anything besides "Unbelievable... well... well..."

I stood, struck by the landscape open to me: where a few minutes ago there had been a smooth, relatively even ice surface only slightly littered with rockfall, now chaos reigned—a heap of pinkish, freshly split blocks strewn over hundreds of square meters.

I felt feverish and was shaking with a strong, continuous tremor. Totally weakened, I dreaded the thought that we had to move through this labyrinth that had grown up in our path.

"Let's go, Volodya, there's no time and nothing to wait

for," Utkin said unexpectedly and out of turn. He said it as though jabbing with a spike into a cavity of a decaying tooth. I cursed him in a hysterical rage—maliciously, venomously, and out of place. At first he looked at me kind-heartedly and cheerfully. But his face suddenly became stern, his eyes severe. Evidently he understood that he would now have to straighten me out, to trample me morally, to subjugate me to his own will.

"Come on, no sniveling! What, do you think I was watching a movie while the mountain was plopping down? Better you should ask how it was for me when the mountain was shooting at me. Thank goodness I wasn't hit. If I had managed to descend two meters lower, I would have had protection over my head."

We made our way through the obstruction. When we came out onto a clean place we saw Kavunenko and Verbovoy three hundred meters from us. They were on their way to help us. However, right now they were standing in place—and in a very strange position.

What had happened was that they had been moving at a distance of about ten steps from each other—Kavunenko in front, Verbovoy in back—not expecting any tricks, at least not there on a rather inoffensive glacier. Suddenly there had been a cracking sound, and almost right under Verbovoy's feet the "earth" opened up, forming a huge two-meter-wide crevasse. We spotted them a moment later, when Volodya Verbovoy, having thrown himself toward Kavunenko, was putting on his pack.

Having noticed us, Verbovoy behaved like Robinson Crusoe upon sighting a ship on the sea. Kavunenko, on the other hand, was like a man turned to stone. "We had already buried you," he said when we approached. "We saw the mountain falling on you! We had contact with the camp just at that moment. So we transmitted to them, 'Shatayev is dead.'" He was silent for several seconds, looking at me astounded and shaking his head. He could not refrain from

Strange Mountains (1957–1963)

making a joke: "Still, the mountain came to Mohammed."

"Well, how are the mountains?" asked Verbovoy.

"I don't understand. Was it an earthquake or something?" Utkin spread his hands in question.

"That's it... A small one... Ten on the scale."

"Ten? In the Caucasus?"

We were late in bringing the news of the distress signal. They already knew. They knew more—the red flare had been set off by Boris Romanov's group, which was evidently in an extremely difficult position. A large rescue team was already on its way.

Soon our two, Balashov and Radimov, descended to the meadow. Because of extensive rockfall, they had not made it to the victims. Three hours later the rescue team came on the evening transmission. The leader announced that the way they were going led to a dead end—the route no longer existed. They had to descend and approach from another side.

We could not rest. The camp was in action. The transmitters were not silent. They were notifying neighboring climbing zones. Regardless of the late hour and the approaching dusk, a helicopter took off and made a run, bringing climbers from the closest base points to the foot of Dombai-Ulgen. Buses loaded with climbers and rescue equipment were racing along the mountain roads, exceeding the speed limit.

On the morning of the third, when the sunrise had just begun to wash away the black of the night, six hundred climbers were on their way. The history of world mountaineering had not known rescue work of a similar scale. The basic group of climbers began ascending from the Bu-Ulgen Gorge. After experiencing great difficulties and taking risks at every minute, they came out on the west side. During the ascent pieces of mountain rock hit the rope six times. It was understandable: Such a large rockfall was brought about by the large number of participants. Somewhere to the right of the exit, at a significant distance, was the group in trouble. A complicated, relatively extensive, dangerous traverse lay ahead. However, it did not become necessary. At the very same time, a vanguard under Vladimir Kavunenko's leadership ventured to ascend from the other side, searching for and breaking through the shortest way to the victims.

At times life appears before us more fantastic than fiction.... We were witnesses to courage that by comparison makes the spiritual strength of [Jack] London's heroes look commonplace.

Romanov and his colleagues—Vorozhishchev and Korotkov—were in bad shape. Yuri Korotkov was especially suffering. They counted about twenty broken bones in him. Injured, weakened, and bricked in by debris from the cliffs, the doctors Romanov and Vorozhishchev cleaned a path with superhuman efforts in order to break out. While doing this they did not leave Yuri Korotkov for one minute and did everything possible under those conditions to sustain his life.

Korotkov did not have, as they say, one unblemished spot—he was one complete injury. They transported him down, obviously not on an ambulance bed with supersprings and not along smooth asphalt. The descent lasted six days. What can one say? What can one add? Only one thing: he held his ground. Below, the doctors said after examining him, "An invalid for life—if he can be saved."

A few years later Yuri Korotkov completed a complicated climb of 5b degree of difficulty and received the title Master of Sports....

The International Climbing Camp on the meadows of Achiktash in the Pamirs.

Official Soviet alpine trainer Vladimir Shatayev.

Oleg Borisenko climbs a wall of ice.

A view of Peak of Communism (7495 m), the highest summit in the USSR, from the slopes of Peak Korzhnevskaya (7105 m).

Khan Tengri (6995 m), in the Tian Shan Range, is not one of the highest summits in the world, but one of the hardest.

Climbers approaching the Caucasus Range through the Adylsu gorge.

An avalanche about to break loose. The first clouds of powder snow are already visible. This is an everyday occurrence on Bezengi (Central Caucasus).

Bezengi (Caucasus): Alpine instructor school near the summit of Mezhigri.

Vladimir Shatayev, standing, in center, surrounded by other climbers.

American climber Alex Bertulis, left, and Soviet colleague V. Grakovich in the North Cascades (Washington state).

V. Grakovich in action.

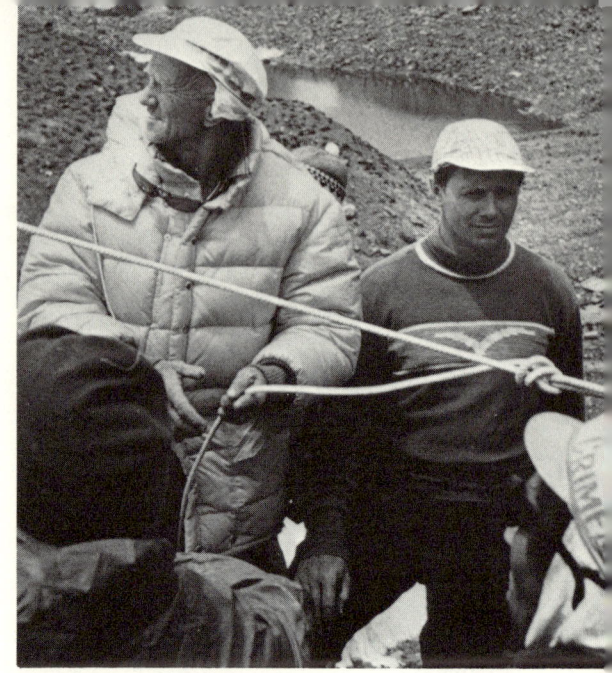

Abalakov, left, and Myslovsky in the Caucasus.

Climbing companions V. Ivanov, left; V. Shatayev, center; and E. Myslovsky.

7. Degrees of Difficulty
(1963–1964)

As I have already mentioned, at the moment of my "visit" to the bergschrund, the radio signal carrying the news of my death was traveling from Kavunenko's group to our camp in the meadow. The news arrived in Moscow with the speed of the telephone. I do not know how it happened. Probably someone called home from Dombai, a settlement two hundred meters from the camp.

Elya had returned to Moscow about a week before, having left me at the camp in my prime and healthy. According to her calculations, I should have been just about ready to return. When the doorbell rang, she flew to the door, expecting to see me. But there instead was a stranger who informed her of my death.

Of course, the sports committee, where she went the next morning, resurrected me. But the experience stayed with her, the trace of despair remained. She had examined and evaluated the meaning of our pastime and had come to the conclusion inevitable under such conditions: Why? Who needs pleasures for which one has to pay with one's life?

When I found out about the misunderstanding, I expected desperate pressure at home, a decisive battle, an ultimatum to give up climbing. But it did not happen.

Having known, if for only a few days, the grief of a loss and the joy of a resurrection, Elvira at first got hold with all fours, as they say, of what is so dear and what is so easy to lose. While waiting for me, she rehearsed from morning to night the impending battle, she tried out in various ways the irresistibility of arguments with which she would begin to convince me. But to all her arguments she soon began to find counterarguments, ones that could not be explained in words, ones that are based not on logic but emotion, and that are inaccessible to the workings of logic. And they arose because Elvira herself in spirit—precisely in spirit and not technically—was already a consummate mountaineer... It happened quickly with her—the law of the spiritual attaction to the mountains worked full force in her.

In short, she battled herself and lost.

We wandered together through the night streets. The grayish lamplight played on the asphalt in splashes, giving the impression that it was strewn with small pieces of glass. Cars raced by with a humming, resilient rustling. Although one anticipated them from behind the line of the highway horizon, for some reason they always appeared suddenly. They flew, rushing and passing each other simply, effortlessly, and just as expectedly but suddenly, disappeared in the huge, sparkling tunnel entrance. There existed in their movement a decisiveness, some combination of goal and action, as if each action at that moment led to the goal, and the goal was the action... I caught myself literally being hypnotized by the indestructible junction of round wheel and tangent asphalt: the eternal point of contact, the beauty and simplicity of this ideal conformation....

Foot and asphalt conform much less. Why should we require a surface to support us on asphalt when, as the tire demonstrates, a point is sufficient? Nature creates its own forms far more perfectly and exactly than man. And if it gives him, instead of wheels, feet with soles, then obviously it is not so that he will walk his whole life across a smooth surface. That is disparity, a disturbance of the balance.

We boarded a half-empty bus. In the aisle was a slender fellow of medium height in a leather jacket unbuttoned and open, with a bluish, pimply face and long hair. Having spread his arms wide, he hung onto both handrails, intentionally but offhandedly, trying to occupy as much space as possible. Obviously, in this position he seemed to himself stronger, more prominent, and more attractive. His intent was obvious, so much so, and so understandable, that Elya and I exchanged glances and laughed quietly.

"Elya, in front of us," I spoke with a guide's voice, "is a conflict of disparity between a personality that recognizes its own vast, simply unending capacity—it is capable of absorbing the whole world into itself—and the mediocre, unnoticed, lost position in which, in reality, it finds itself."

"You laugh in vain," Elya said. "I don't judge him. He wants to be worth something, to mean something. And most important, he wants to be conscious that he is worth something, means something. Maybe, because of this he will go to any length."

"And will he go into the mountains?"

"If he's smart, he'll go!"

It seemed to me that now was an appropriate time to tell her about what had been on the tip of my tongue for more than a day, something I had not yet made up my mind to start talking about, considering that ill-fated day she had experienced.

"That means I'm not a fool? Then I will give the others my consent."

She immediately felt that a serious and unpleasant proposal was to follow. Biting her lip, she threw me a sharp, anxious look and, controlling herself, asked quietly, stretching out every word, "What consent? To what?"

"We want to go to Ushba."

My friends with families had one advantage: they could, so

to speak, deceive their wives, lull their anxieties. They could convince them that the climb was trivial and did not present any danger.

Elya was already sufficiently erudite about climbing to understand what it meant to climb Ushba. She turned white and did not answer immediately. Then she asked, "Who's 'we'?"

"Volodya Kavunenko, Volodya Verbovoy, and Edik Myslovsky."

"That's very flattering—to appear in the company of such strong and significant mountaineers. I understand. And Ushba is ripe—in big mountaineering it can't be avoided. Only what's it to you, big mountaineering?"

"Elya..."

"Okay, don't answer... I know that the conversation is useless. You won't change anything, you won't stop. It's just that it's difficult for me, Volodya."

"Elya, that's not all of it."

"I feel it. A new route, I suppose?"

If only it were that! I thought. "No. We want to go in the winter."

She looked at me for several minutes as if my face had been covered with wool right before her eyes. Then she said, "Nobody has thought of that up to now! Spineless creatures, envisioning themselves as titans of mountaineering. They've hardly clothed themselves in the first class."

"That doesn't mean anything. By the way. Kavunenko has been a Master for three years now. But that's not the point. One cannot live one's whole life looking to authorities. They've rubber-stamped mountaineering. Everything has been discovered, everything has been done... At times people qualify for all the athletic regalia without having said a single word of their own. Mountaineering is not simply six degrees of difficulty. Above all, it is discovery. It is daring."

Actually, who are we to be so daring? Unknown first-classers, who are supposed to break through to Master by classical, beaten trails. How dare we jump across a class and act in the realm accessible only to famous masters?

We bowed to the names, lived under the feet of their authority with a subconscious conviction that their achievements were the highest goal we could realize, and possibly only in our dreams. It seemed to us that we still had not even reached the limit of current climbing achievement, much less the unexplored horizons that stretched beyond. In short, immaturity still spoke in us...

o

Mountaineering is divided into four classes of technical difficulty.... *Technical climbs* entail difficult rock on relatively low summits. *High-altitude technical climbs* combine difficult rock with altitude. On *high-altitude climbs* the main factor to overcome is altitude itself. Finally, *traverses* involve crossing several summits running. Separate from all of this is rock climbing—now it is not even called mountaineering—where athletes display the pure technique of solving difficult rock problems, and where the goal is not to ascend a summit but to conquer a difficult wall in the best time.

Climbers, of course, can dedicate themselves solely to any one of these types. At times it happens. There are Masters of Sports who were brought up exclusively in the Caucasus. Not having been in the Pamirs a single time, they work only in the class of technical climbs. But most often a climber is many-sided. Even if, say, high-altitude climbs are to his liking, all the same he goes on climbs of other types from time to time.

Ushba is a technical climb. It is on the short list of the most difficult summits on earth, and its ascent crowns the academic mastery of a climber. At the same time, the peak is less attractive precisely because it is too academic and popular. Every climber on the road to serious climbing will certainly test himself on Ushba's walls, for they have become the traditional touchstone, the test of virtuosity.

Despite all its extreme difficulty, climbs of Ushba are as a rule successful. I think how many good reputations this tricky mountain has confirmed thanks to the unique psychology of climbers. The glory of Ushba is such that the mountain in essence excludes chance ascents. Only athletes who have matured can pose a threat to it. An inexperienced climber would prefer the Peak of Communism because for him the difficulties of altitude are invisible, nearly incomprehensible, while Ushba is frightening just to look at.

I repeat, only strong climbers lay claim to it. They succeed in climbing it mainly because doing so is their "dissertation defense," which is preceded by a lengthy, painstaking preparation. . . . All the same, Ushba is traveled like the lobby of a subway station. Our hearts probably rebelled against this too. The pretense of being discoverers in mountain travel had ripened in us—we did not want to be ordinary or to repeat what had already been done so many times.

"It's not accessible in winter!" This self-evident truth swallowed discussion.

Of all the obstacles and difficulties encountered during our Ushba epic, which lasted two years and took the life of one of us, the most difficult was our asking ourselves, "Why?" Daring, I think, is the highest degree of difficulty. Having asked ourselves this question, we had taken the most valuable, the most difficult, the bravest step.

Even the beginning was unusual. Winter is winter, even in the Caucasus: the snow came down, covering the woods and whitening the mountains to their base. Approaches to the two-horned mountain had to be made on cross-country skis. After a six-hour trip we were at the Nemetskie Nochevki—the starting point of the climb.

The farther back you have to crane your neck, the more frightening the route when seen from below. And this, as is known, depends not so much on its height as its steepness. When my eyes surveyed the slope of our chosen route and came to the highest visible point, my neck literally rested on my back. Ushba's threatening "face" rises even more because the largest part of this mountain stands isolated. It does not merge with the ridge, does not grow out of it, but sticks up, stepping lightly away from its neighbors. Therefore all its slopes are clearly visible and their steepness is striking.

Now Ushba stood cheerless, covered in ice, white in color but gray in mood. This deathliness oppressed us and beat down our climbing excitement.

We chose the traditional and most logical way—from the north side, a traverse of the north and south summits. I had the counter number 450. I do not remember who of us six had the lowest number, but even if mine was the last, that means 444 people had been on Ushba before us. Of those, more than half had gone by this route. We could memorize the route like a poem, however, without really knowing what awaited us.

Winter changes everything. Like a new housewife, it creates an interior according to its own taste. The symbols on the map that designated areas of avalanche danger were not only worthless, but the opposite—disorienting. One should now move them to other places unknown to anyone. In addition their quantity increased greatly. Winter drew a route with new crevasses, snow flags, cornices...

What else awaited us? Forty-below weather, with penetrating winds whose only constancy is to be inconstant, whose direction changes unexpectedly, illogically, sharply, contrarily. Movement on the mountain would be blind, by feel, because the cliff cracks and crevices necessary for hammering in pitons would be plastered with snow and covered with ice. In addition, the short winter days would limit working time and lengthen the duration of the climb. These general, rather well-known aspects of the climb could be predicted. We also assumed there would be other factors that would not come to mind.

All the same, we foresaw some things. We even took a

broom, to clean away the snow while we looked for places to hammer in pitons. And the main thing: Kavunenko and I went out to Tsaritsyno all January and climbed on the towers without gloves. Our hands had to get used to the cold.

We set off on the route in three groups of two. Kavunenko and I were in the lead; Eduard Myslovsky and Vladimir Verbovoy were second; and Leonid Polyakov and Lev Dobrovolsky were third. Kavunenko was the leader of the climb.

Our backpacks broke all records this time. No matter how we economized, no matter how we limited ourselves to the most necessary items, no matter how carefully we weighed the food—literally to the gram—the weight of each of our loads surpassed thirty-three kilograms. That's to be expected—increased reserves of warm clothes, standby equipment, food—the climb would be lengthy.

"Never mind," Kavunenko joked. "It'll be easier for us to stay on the ground."

The "boring" Shkheldinsky Glacier soon ended. The climbing then became "fun," for we had come out on the Ushba Icefall. Reminding us of the skeleton of a huge animal, the cracked, whitish-gray strip rose steeply, squeezed between cliffs about two hundred meters apart. The glacier made continuous, threatening noises—somewhere seracs were being destroyed and ice blocks were breaking off and sliding downward.

Here the glacier, having overcome a gigantic rock threshold, breaks apart at the step and farther on breaks up some more, bending and flowing down a steep channel.

This icefall is a classic of ice climbing, the most difficult terrain on the mountain. You do not find such a quantity of crevasses anywhere else on the route. There is no guarantee that at the moment you are on the icefall still another crevasse will not appear, and that precisely between your right foot and left foot.

Kavunenko went first. Because of the extreme steepness, he had to move more and more on all fours. At times he

Degrees of Difficulty (1963–1964) 111

reminded us of a soldier who would not take a step until he had tested the place with a mine detector. When possible he tried to go around the crevasses in a reasonable way, leaving a "rabbit" track behind us. Unfortunately, it was not always possible. Some of the crevasses stretched from one side of the icefall to the other, forcing us to find a narrower place and, belaying carefully, jump.

Kavunenko went around a mighty serac. As if poured from glazed earthenware, it came down onto the cone of an ice stump, fluted with icicles and strangely crowned with a semihorizontal slab that looked like the peak of a modern building. The serac looked like a hammer. Skirting it on the right, Volodya came out under an overhang, stopped under the very edge, and began to cut a step. He looked up warily several times, contemplating the unreliability of such a roof, but progress was impossible any other way. He hurried, becoming more convinced of his premonition with every passing second. In order to get clear of the perched block of ice, he increased the length of his next three steps. On the fourth one he straightened up to his full height and sighed in relief.

I was just about to cross the same section when he shouted "Wait!" As he stared intently at the slab, it collapsed.

Kavunenko's mystical foresight was a subject of humor for a long time afterward. He assured us of his ability to destroy and build with the help of a glance. Later, when he was tired of making fun, he admitted that he had experienced a very unpleasant feeling, having noticed that the peak was cracked and was holding on only by its word of honor.

Everything has an end, including the icefall, although we had ceased to believe it. Eventually, it led us out onto the great Ushba plateau.

The eye rested easily on the serene, white plain. But we knew that danger lay hidden beneath this smooth, pacifying snow surface. There were not many crevasses, but those that existed were masked by the deep snow and hard to recognize.

The going became more difficult. Having exerted ourselves greatly on the icefall, we were now walking at the limits of our strength. The backpack bent me over lower and lower, and my legs disappeared up to my knees. Every five or six steps I stopped to take a breath, but I didn't know which was better, to move or to stand. The thermometer showed thirty-four degrees (Celsius) below, and there on the plateau the high-altitude wind wandered unrestricted. As soon as one stopped one began to freeze. Now I took the lead. It was time to relieve Kavunenko, who had broken trail for us in the most difficult places.

The workday ended on the Ushba Pillow. This rectangular "table," about two hundred meters long and twenty to thirty meters wide, covered with a slightly convex snow-firn layer, became our place for the night.

The route description stated that the Pillow, as a rule, was easy to cross because the winds blow away freshly fallen snow and leave a compact, "rolled" thin crust of ice over the snow, which is a pleasure to walk on. But that happens in the summer. In winter there is enough snow to cover the Pillow no matter how hard the winds try.

We crossed the Pillow, drowning in the snow and breaking trail, and at the base of an ice slope we dug a cave. Although the hands on my watch showed 7:00 P.M., it had already been dark for a long time. Such is winter.

Volodya Verbovoy prepared dinner, and Kavunenko, stuffing down the farina with jam, feverishly, as if delirious, mumbled compliments to him. "You, Verbovoy," he said, licking his spoon, "are an invader, a usurper, the captor of my heart. I will not part with you until the grave! Do you hear, Shatayev? Let's make a bond with him for life. Now I won't even go to the Central Russian heights without him."

"Okay, you won't buy it!" Kavunenko continued. "All the same, you'll prepare breakfast yourself. And if you want a culinary class, come visit me in Moscow for pilaf and beer."

"Cold beer?" Myslovsky asked, shivering. The stove

brought warmth to the cave and, finally, stiff from the cold, our bodies thawed. But the memory of the sensation, which is usually short, was still alive in us.

"Well, no, perhaps I'll boil it."

"Normal people are sitting right now somewhere in a bar," said Leonid, "swigging beer, eating bream—"

"And cursing life out of boredom," Verbovoy interrupted. "And you... look at yourself in a mirror... you have the happiness of farina and hot tea written all over you."

"Exactly, Volodya," continued Kavunenko. "God gives people farina in reward for ordeals. And for subjection to the winter of Ushba He adds jam."

"I think, Volodya," Verbovoy said in Kavunenko's tone, "having returned home, we will receive the moral right to be nourished on farina alone, at least until the first payday."

For some reason, Volodya's "having returned home" struck me. The friendly laughter summoned forth in my heart a strange, pointless, and momentary, superstitious protest: "We still have to return home!" I did not feel like discussing Verbovoy's proposal to leave a small part of the food in the cave, although his idea was correct. According to our plan, we were not supposed to come back, since for a complete traverse we should descend from the south summit to Svanetya. But the Svanskie slopes of Ushba are avalanche hazards even in the summer. In the winter, and moreover in bad weather, the risk increases many times. There was at least a fifty-fifty chance that a descent along the ascent route was in store for us. If so, then Verbovoy was right. Even if we descended into Svanetya, starvation would not threaten us—after all, we would be descending to people.

That's how it was. But the soberness of reason betrayed me. I did not want to take part in the necessary and sensible discussion of the alternatives.

The next day at dawn we were already on our feet (more exactly, on our crampons). The steep ice slope led us to Nastenko's Cliffs, which are not considered very difficult and are not dangerous by mountaineering standards. But about twenty years ago, the climber Nastenko, having decided to conquer Ushba by himself, fell here and perished.

The cliffs stretched upward for about one hundred meters. Every piton was a problem to hammer in. The crevices, covered with ice and snow, were at times no easier to find than a white mushroom in the forest. But even having discovered and cleaned such a mushroom, one does not always succeed in determining at a glance whether it is edible. So it was with pitons. Sometimes one has to extract a piton already beaten in because it is too loose and would be dangerous to put a load on it. A piton is reliable when it "sings" as it is going into the body of the cliff. Even so, everything turned out successfully for us there, and we covered the hundred meters rather quickly.

Beyond the cliffs a view appeared that was threatening, yet striking in its uniqueness—a huge, tilted ice slab. It was so bewitching that at first, having forgotten about our climbing task, we did not experience the slightest bit of fear; we became only observers. But when we came to our senses, we became uneasy and remembered that we had to cross it.

Had it been horizontal, the ice slab, which stretched for three hundred meters and was smooth and polished, would have made an excellent high-mountain skating rink. But one could not skate on it—one could only slide down it. Its glassy transparency, it seemed, permitted us to examine the deep deathly sullen interior of Ushba.

It was clear that without step cutting and pitons one could not take a step here. Even so, I tried to cross it with crampons, but I could have done as well on a marble floor. The ice was so hard that my crampons only scratched it.

In the summer we would have been able to cut steps with five or six blows of the axe. But now every step required twenty-two to twenty-five blows. The unusual structure of the winter ice caused it to split off in dinner plates of different sizes, which sped down the slope, threatening to injure those working below. They covered themselves with their rucksacks, but their unprotected hands often received painful knocks.

Then there was the matter of the old pitons left behind by previous climbers. It's a pity one cannot use them. They sat in disorderly nests, graphic evidence that the ice was indeed flowing. Originally beat in perpendicular to the slope, they were now almost parallel to it, their heads just barely clearing the ice.

At six o'clock in the evening, Kavunenko and I were standing one and a half meters from the summit ridge, if *standing* means fastened to steep, almost vertical cliffs and supporting oneself by the toes of one's boots on barely marked ledges. Not even a tightrope walker could have kept his balance on the ridge itself, which was so sharp that Volodya, upon seeing it, said, "Don't cut your hand."

A little bit below us on a narrow, semi-inclined shelf, which actually provided a place to sit, Myslovsky, Polyakov, and Dobrovolsky had situated themselves, tied, as we were, to pitons. And at the very bottom, where the slab met the wall, Volodya Verbovoy was on the last ice step. Leaning back as much as the runner from a small piece of line would allow, he was ready to ascend.

The weather had pleased us more that morning than now. I had crawled out of our cave and been pleasantly surprised by a sharp warming. The mercury column in the thermometer had climbed high and showed minus ten. During the day it went up persistently, and toward evening it had reached five below.

It was frighteningly quiet. Snow fell in huge flakes, slowly, smoothly, as in a theater at a Christmas performance. The day ended, but from our place the dotted line left by our ice axes was still clearly visible, stretching from Verbovoy to the lower edge of the slab. We had worked well at destroying its beauty.

The silence lasted a long time—the whole evening and

night and the next day. It did not betoken anything; it was not the calm before the storm; nature was not planning to play a trick on us. Even so, nature is not given to changelessness. It is dynamic; everything changes unavoidably. At every instant, somewhere, something is changing. The stone had been there for thousands of years, but at precisely that moment, time ran out for one of its attributes and began for another.

The rock was about fifteen meters to the right of us and a little above. In size and form it resembled a box for a fancy cake. It was exactly above Volodya Verbovoy, and you could measure the distance with the length of a climbing rope.

Volodya was wearing a helmet. But when we all yelled "rock" as loudly as we could, he lifted his head and the rock struck him in the face. We nurtured hope for a few minutes. But when Myslovsky descended, he saw that Volodya was dead.

It was completely dark and quiet, as before. Kavunenko and I turned our backs to each other as much as was possible. Nobody uttered a word, unable to break the funereal silence of the mountains. Only after half an hour did Kavunenko ask hoarsely, not knowing to whom he was turning, "Did you check carefully? Maybe..."

"Yes," Myslovsky answered from below.

It wasn't worth thinking about a descent or any kind of movement now—you could not make out your own hands. Everyone remained in their places.

The situation of the three below us was not easy. Their "living space" allowed them only to pull the sleeping bag over their legs. They did that without worrying about the fate of the four-person down bag. They put it on right over their crampons. Kavunenko and I only dreamed of such "luxury." For us, even that comfort was impossible.

It was excruciatingly cold. My legs, especially the right one, were freezing to the point of a pain in my heart. The "physical exercise" lasted all night: until dawn we shifted from one foot to the other, danced around, jumped up and down as much as possible, and slapped ourselves on our sides. But it did not help much.

The stove lay in my rucksack. One cannot say that I forgot about it—I simply considered it a thing that, at the moment, had perhaps only one meaning: to make my load heavier. But, as is known, Pinocchio's father was sometimes warmed by a painted hearth, since cold, as well as hunger, is very conducive to the growth of the imagination. At first I imagined the burning stove—just like that, abstractly. And then I imagined how it would look here on the wall.

It was about 1:00 A.M. when Kavunenko and I decided to realize this enterprise. Our numbed hands would not obey. We had to spend a lot of time getting it, attaching it to a piton, and pouring fuel. Having taken off our mittens, we were risking our last warmth. And if we did not succeed in lighting it? But we did—the stove was burning.

In the morning the misfortune became clear again. It was as if he was standing, leaning out on the loop, his hands hanging down and his head thrown back as though he were watching us.

Our spirits were tormented by a thought: if we had not yelled that ill-fated "Rock" the piece of rock would have fallen on his helmet—it might have saved his life. I recalled the incident with the logs that I had heard in camp several years ago. The situation was similar; although now, ten years later, evaluating the circumstances more calmly, I think that it was impossible to foresee such a turn of events. However, this thought has always been with me, even to this day.

Contacting the camp by radio, we informed them of the accident. They suggested that we descend, leaving the corpse in place. The camp sent out a rescue group to get Verbovoy's body. However, the question was not discussed. I do not remember whether anyone even mentioned a word about it. The decision was accepted silently and unanimously. We took him down off the belay carefully, supporting him from behind so that he would not fall. He had become stiff and did not bend. We placed him in a sack and dragged him down. It is difficult work even for people with fresh strength. But we were in that state of physical exhaustion where strengths are gathered from unknown sources.

We conducted the descent in a precise, orderly, and thorough way. The most difficult section was on the Ushba Icefall. Shaliko Margiani's rescue team met us below the icefall and took over further transport of the body.

Thus ended the first sad episode of our winter conquest of Ushba. The story would continue the following year, in 1965.

In the summer of 1964 I completed two serious and difficult ascents in the Caucasus, conquering the summits Dalar and Dvuzubka, and I completed the requirements for the title Master of Sports. In that same season, my first trip abroad, to Italy, took place. On the representative team, besides myself, were A. Kaspin (leader), V. Kizel, A. Kuznetsov, V. Kavunenko, K. Kletsko, and G. Agranovsky. We returned home with the pleasant knowledge that our notes remained on difficult Alpine summits.

8. The Winter Route
(1965)

Once again we were on the Ushba Pillow. I felt as though we had not left the cave, that the past year, saturated and packed to the limit, had not occurred. Yet the cave was not the same, and even the makeup of the group was different. Only Kavunenko and I remained from the previous team. With us now were Masters of Sport: Boris Studenin from Alma-Ata; Vladimir Bezlyudny, a Muscovite from the trade union sports society Truda; and Victor Tur from the Moscow volunteer sports society Spartak, as well as Nikolai Radimov, a Muscovite of the first rating.

It now seemed to me as though what had happened had not yet happened, as though the horror we had experienced yet awaited us. While still in Moscow, I had been afraid of these psychological recurrences.

The hole we dug for the cave left bloody calluses, even on our accustomed mountaineers' hands. A crevasse about fifteen centimeters wide crossed the cave. Its depth was such that the sound of a falling object simply did not reach us. We called it the "garbage chute" because we threw in cans, cellophane from food, leftovers. Although the crevasse was clearly too narrow to be dangerous, its chill remained in our hearts.

The sorrow had not left me during the entire year. Even the trip to Italy had not distracted me from thoughts of Ushba. The final days before departure were tedious and drawn-out; I urged the days to pass and dreamed of riding the train from Moscow to Nalchik. The winter Ushba remained an unsolved problem, one made all the more intriguing by the increasing certainty that solving it was within our power.

Success is possible where there is no self-deception, where there exists an honest approach to the goal. Thus we spoke honestly among ourselves: The accident had occurred because we had brought old preconceptions to what were mostly new conditions, because we had applied standard techniques to a winter route. Winter placed us in qualitatively new climbing conditions, conditions in which the question of safety could not be decided by mountaineering skill alone. A method was needed, a special tactic of safety.

I spent the whole night in a slow, nightmarish semisleep, and in the morning I said to Kavunenko, "I dreamed of Verbovoy."

He looked at me in surprise and answered sullenly, "I did too."

If telepathic communication indeed exists, then it is probably established between Kavunenko and myself. It's understandable—there is no better communication than a rope. When moving we interact silently. Only sometimes do we throw out two necessary phrases: "Slack" and "Up rope." I do not know whether a skipper can talk to the helm, but a climber, like a mine sweeper, cannot talk while working.

The weather was excellent. Kolya Radimov and Vitya Tur crawled out of the cave. The good visibility allowed them to examine the remainder of the route. The details—alas!—were not comforting. Ushba was covered with an icy coat of mail, from which a cold wind blew that froze the heart more than the body.

They told us at breakfast that they felt bad and could go no

The Winter Route (1965)

farther. It was probably so. But even if it were not so, I would not begin to judge them. Sobriety is not condemnable. Sobriety is the best human quality, although the romantic scorns it.

Even if it were not so, I would say: Radimov and Tur did not limit anyone, they did not lead anybody on. They added up their strengths and, comparing them with the forthcoming difficulties, decided that the climb did not suit them.

Even if it were not so, I would say: they behaved honestly and courageously, for they were not afraid of kitchen judgments. In general, they did not concern themselves with what others thought of them. They did not begin to violate their own hearts for the sake of posing as fearless heroes. And this is sobriety—the best of human qualities.

They went down, we up. More exactly, of those who had decided to force their way to the summit only Kavunenko and I set out at that time. Climbing in separate small teams was the essence of our new climbing tactic; I say "new," although this method has long been known to and used by climbers. And yet we did not copy the "bicycle"; we reinvented it. We reassembled dozens of complex, wonderful, imperfect versions that wouldn't work—until, finally, we selected the single, best, optimal one. What do you do if it turns out to be a "bicycle"?

I speak of this in detail because I consider it necessary to emphasize an important boundary in a climber's life: If he begins to be concerned more about questions of strategy and tactics than about technique, it means that mountaineering maturity has come upon him.

And thus, Kavunenko and I set off upward and the team of Studenin and Bezlyudny remained at the bivouac site. The method was as follows: we would work out a section of the route, including the ice slab, prepare it for the climb, and come back down in order to approach the next section with fresh strength the following day. In this way the second group would not be subjected to danger (I have already mentioned that from the axes of the upper group fly fragments that can injure the ones below). In addition, we could work with lighter loads—our rucksacks remained in the cave. Finally, we would approach the most difficult section (the summit ridge), which followed the ice slab, with a reasonable reserve of strength.

It is true that there arose an ethical misunderstanding. While still in camp, when this tactic was being discussed, Boris Studenin said, "Perhaps you will pull us to the summit on a sled." But both Studenin and Bezlyudny understood; they could be annoyed only that they were not the first but the second team. One has to sacrifice pride for the sake of general success and safety. We promised not to hang perlon and to leave only pitons and steps.

On that day we prepared two hundred meters of the slab. The ice was now even harder than last year. At least two hundred and fifty blows of the hammer were required for an ice screw. At the same time, before a piton would go in as far as the head, we had to strike it about two hundred times. In the summer, fifty to sixty blows are sufficient. We took a piece of red material with us, and in order to distinguish our own pitons from those of others we marked them with a red ribbon—they attracted the eye even from far away.

The next day, we set off two hours before the second team and came out on the ridge that much ahead of them. We moved slowly and carefully, as if crossing a beam erected two kilometers above the ground, with the difference that the ridge, unlike a horizontal beam, was at an incline.

I have been amazed at how orchestra players, with their heads buried in the music, contrived to see the conductor's hands. Did they not have a third eye in their temple? Now I myself acquired this temple vision, a vision nourished by nervous energy and devouring it all.

I shattered the snow-ice edge of the ridge with my ice hammer and beat in a belay piton. I watched my hands, of course, but I also vigilantly followed my partner, who was about fifteen meters from me. It was essential not to break this visual connection, even for a second. If Kavunenko fell to the right, then at the same moment I would have to throw myself to the left. A note played at the wrong time in the orchestra grates on the ear of a music lover. A "note" not played at the right time by me would cost us our lives.

The ridge went slowly. There were continuous snow cornices, outstretched and white, like the wings of a sea gull hanging over a precipice. Alas, there was no guarantee of their firmness. With each one I waited for it to disappear beneath my feet. In places, where there was no possibility at all of walking along the ridge, we descended a few meters and went along the wall.

The four of us reached the highest point of the north tower together. But this was only part of the traverse, and it was a little early to rejoice. We still had to descend along the southern slope, cross the col, and ascend the south tower. The weather became bad—a wind came up and it began to snow. There was neither the time nor the conditions for admiring the panorama. Leaving a note, we immediately descended to the col, chopped out an ice platform under the slope, and set up a bivouac.

Mountaineers call Ushba Col a chimney. Even in good weather strong, changing, whirling winds wander through it. In bad weather it is hell there. Our position was dismal, like the dark space under a fence. One's legs, like those of a parachutist on his first jump, failed just from one look at the prospect. I had never seen a ridge with such a mass of cornices. The most frightening of them, x-shaped, spread like wings to the left and to the right, were reminiscent of the upper part of a Latin x. They rose before us like x's and y's in an equation with many unknowns. Not knowing where it was better and safer to cross them—to the left or to the right—we finally went at random along the supported middle. But the shallow between the wings might have been displaced from the vertical axis of the ridge, the right wing could have grown out of the left or vice versa, and then the smallest load would have been sufficient for the entire structure to crash down.

It took us five hours to cross two hundred meters of the col, and toward midday, without food and almost without rest, we started the assault on the south tower. There was no rest on it either, for the cliff wall shoots up at close to sixty degrees.

Kavunenko scaled it first. When he reached the summit he was worn out. It seemed there was no strength left in him even to rejoice. He stood with his chest leaning on his axe, his head hung low. I looked him in the face. But no, in it was the radiance that breaks through only in moments of rare happiness. His eyes laughed with a child's naive laugh; it was unusual to see him so open and vulnerable.

At that point there should have been a half-hour rest, but it was impossible to stand there an extra minute. The wind blew with a long, continuous, ever-rising note, as if singing it in one breath. The snow struck the face as if it were sand. The only vista was an unbroken expanse of seemingly boiling milk.

We did not find the summit note because the cairn was buried somewhere in the snow. Volodya, in spite of his fatigue, did not decline the honorable right of the leader to write a note. He scratched a few lines with his reluctant hand, placed the piece of paper in a food can, dug up rocks in the snow, and erected his own cairn.

The bad weather had already started on the north summit, and when we descended there, it had already been clear that the way to Svanetya was closed to us. The danger of avalanches coming down this side was so great that a traverse was the equivalent of suicide. Yet having decided to return along the ascent route, we had left our rucksacks in the tents in order to progress more easily along the col. Now, as it turned out, we were in the most distressing situation.

When we came down from the south tower it was ten P.M.

The Winter Route (1965)

Although the weather had calmed and there was even a narrow crescent moon lighting the mountains, it was still dark. To spend the night there... But how? What would we spread out? What would we use to cover ourselves? How would we keep warm? Perhaps an ice axe under the head and a hammer on top? Everything was in the rucksacks. Like it or not, we would have to make our way back to the tents. The same difficult two hundred meters covered with cornices led to them. Now we would have to cross it blindly.

Kavunenko could no longer lead so I had to assume the role myself. We discussed the system of movement and decided as follows: I would go out one rope length, find a suitable platform, prepare it, organize the belay, and bring the others across. I would reconnoiter and prepare the next forty meters and again bring the others across, and so on.

In my right hand was an axe; in my left, a flashlight. I sat on top of the sharp col, trying to illuminate the mountains with a pocket light. The rope stretched out behind me—I would have to hang from it when I flew into a precipice. I lit up the nearest meter, felt it from all sides with my axe, and searched for a piton that we might have pounded in several hours before. I tried to learn by heart everything I saw, since in order to move I needed free hands. That meant I had to put the light away in my pocket and remember where everything was. Thus I moved, meter after meter, amazed at the unusual length of the rope. I had always thought that it was forty meters, but it turned out to be kilometers and kilometers!...

Finally, the rope was out, yet a place to bring the group had still not appeared. Then the ridge suddenly made a small zigzag a little to the right and down a meter. I went down and felt that it was possible to stand on my feet. A suitable platform. If I worked it with an axe, perhaps a ruble would fit. It would be difficult to dance, but maybe eight soles would fit. If only it were not a cornice... But, it didn't seem to be. Then I needed to set up a belay, a familiar rote chore. I was afraid of this familiarity. I was afraid of involuntarily, subconsciously relaxing my vigilance, which one is especially disposed to do when extremely tired.... I was afraid of that tolerance which leads to a reduction in safety. In such a matter the only acceptable percentage of certainty is one hundred; ninety-nine is a crime.

The moon, as if out of spite, moved behind a cloud for what seemed a long time. With the help of the flashlight I found a ledge. Was it ice or rock covered with ice? At another time, kicking it several times with my foot, I would have pronounced it solid. There would have been no grounds for not trusting my judgment. Now I feared one thing—that I would accept desire as reality. It would be better, as they say, to blow on cold soup. I rejected the ledge and decided to pound in a piton.

The cursed darkness—I was not a carpenter and not capable of working with a hammer "by heart." However, it turned out not too badly. Out of two hundred blows, only one landed on my hand. But that was enough for the moon behind the clouds to flare up like the sun.

Everything was ready. The end of work and the beginning of the play on nerves. On a signal from me a dim eye of a light separated from the slope of the south tower and tossed chaotically from side to side, in circles, and in zigzags. At times it froze for a long time or disappeared altogether. It was not clear from appearances whether it was coming closer or not. Although I actually knew it was drawing nearer, I stood with the rope. When the light beam suddenly fell downward, I seized it and braced myself in anticipation of a jerk. But everything was in order. The beam rose again and began its dance.

Finally Boris Studenin was beside me. Then, just as slowly, squeezing my heart, Volodya Bezlyudny and Kavunenko arrived. The temperature was lower than thirty below. But I did not feel it, even when stationary. On the contrary, I was constantly bathed in heat—psychological energy works no less than mechanical.

The Winter Route (1965)

All were together and I went ahead again...

It occurred to me that Elya was not sleeping now and was thinking of me. Her waiting was no less torturous and tense than what I was experiencing belaying my friends. Only hers was an even greater uncertainty and would be stretched out for many days. I imagined myself in her place and suddenly thought, Judging by everything, I would not be able to avoid such an experience myself, perhaps in the very near future — she was acquiring the technique of mountaineering very quickly and well.

At times, human experiences look more dramatic to outsiders than to those who are experiencing them. Such probably was the case then. I had no feeling that I was at the limit of human strength. It seemed that the limit was always a little way off. A little would pass and a little more, but either the limit receded or I simply did not know how far away it actually was. And this not knowing was the most agonizing. You experience something similar in a dentist's chair when the dentist's drill hits a nerve. Later, when you sort it out, you understand that it is not the pain itself that is so agonizing — you can stand that — but the fear that it will become even worse. In short... the greatest negative in life is fear. Goethe's Mephistopheles is probably fear itself; whoever conquers him is happy. Ultimately, we climb in order to derive happiness. Why, then, the question "Why do you go into the mountains?"

I was afraid it would be worse when I went out on the second and third rope lengths. But on the fourth and fifth, with the light of the moon peeping out, I saw that the north summit was but a stone's throw away. And then it became clear: The most difficult part was behind me.

Up to now I have not yet had to cross my limit on a single route, although it is possible that I have approached it in earnest more than once. I therefore think that all of my climbs have been within my strength, within the limits of my personal capabilities. I have only gone where I felt I was capable.

People say to me, "Even if you know your own strength, it's unknown how much strength is necessary to master an unfamiliar climb. Can you determine below whether it is within your capabilities or not?" You can and you must. In this lies the essence of what it means to be an experienced climber—intuition. Your eye becomes practiced at visually evaluating the route. With every climb comes an ever-increasing objective knowledge of your own physical and spiritual strengths. Genuine maturity in a climber is crowned precisely by a sense that tells him what he is up to and what he is not. And until he acquires such maturity this question must be decided for him by others—in the most strict, instructional manner. There is no democracy here, and there cannot be, for in mountaineering it is immoral. Once again I say: Only this type of mountaineering has the right to exist.

The rules of mountaineering, which I subsequently happened to help develop, are aimed at making this sport as safe as possible without dulling the acute sense of risk. Of course, the rules are far from ideal. They do not prevent all accidents nor guarantee complete freedom from them. But they are continually being polished by growing mountaineering experience. And their correction originates not from behind office desks, but on such cols as this one.

But, I repeat, these rules are a long way from perfection. Part of their inadequacy is that they are not strict enough concerning the question of who is to be permitted to do what. I have already said once in these pages that a climber has a right only to those climbs that he can complete with a large reserve of endurance. In the rules this is reflected as a basic idea. And still it demands special emphasis. It should be embodied in an even stricter, uncompromising form.

I imagined myself in Elya's place, and her in mine. And I felt terrible in advance. More and more women claim the right to attempt this summit. When the first of them received permission and started up, the legislators of mountaineering had doubt in their hearts: Was this right? Since then a few women have ascended the summit of Ushba. Of course, all of them went with a large male group. But there is a dangerous tendency in this: women will also get used to the idea that Ushba is a crowning and necessary step in their mountaineering education. I thought then, a little time will pass, and Elya will be approaching in earnest this level of "higher education" and will not for anything want to decline it. I imagined her here on the col, or on the Ushba Icefall. In the summer it's another matter—simpler of course—but all the same—was it really in principle within women's strengths?

Toward two o'clock that night the col was behind us for good. Five rope lengths—five hours. Then another five hours awake in the tent—we were so tired we could not fall asleep.

In the morning we examined the tracks we had "drawn" and were horrified: several hours earlier we had been saved by none other than a miracle. One of the platforms onto which I had brought the fellows turned out to be a cornice. Judging by how it was trampled down, we had felt very sure on it, but the cornice looked weak. It's incomprehensible how it held us four.

The descent went normally, if you do not consider a certain adventure involving Volodya Kavunenko. During a small traverse of a wall, he went behind a bend. Bezlyudny fed out the rope to him blindly and a little too slowly. His timing was bad, and Kavunenko was pulled off the mountain. But with a good belay and by his own mastery, he flew like a pendulum about ten meters and landed happily on his feet without a single injury, escaping with a slight fright. . . .

With this, ended the winter conquest of Ushba.

Now in 1976, I cannot refrain from emphasizing the uniqueness of this climb: Ten years have passed, and to this day our "winter path" has not been repeated.

9. The Moral Aspect of the Theory of Probability

(1971)

I could not sleep. The knocking and the rocking—the monotony of the train—did not lull me to sleep. On the contrary: it was infuriating, like the sounds of a clock intensified to hammer blows by insomnia. Elya must have been having a pleasant dream. The lights fleeting behind the window caught her smile. She was happy, like a graduating high school student who has been accepted into a university—the forthcoming difficulties did not worry her. Elya had been included in a group to climb the Peak of Communism. This seemed the most important thing to her now...

Together with us in the compartment were the Master of Sports of International Class Eduard Myslovsky and a stranger, a gray-haired mathematics teacher, Boris Aleksandrovich. He was a strange old man: too attentive and too tactful. Every time a conversation would start among ourselves he would leave the compartment, and upon returning he would knock and ask whether he was disturbing us. Finally Elya said that we had no secrets; on the contrary, we enjoyed his company. "In that case," our neighbor answered, "I would be interested in listening to your climbing discussions."

The Moral Aspect of the Theory of Probability (1971)

Boris Aleksandrovich, as he himself expressed it, was going into the past—a friend of his from the front lived in Osh. After the war they had corresponded for twenty-five years but had not managed to see each other. Now the possibility had finally arisen.

Feeling that I would not fall asleep, I took a book and went out into the corridor. After about five minutes Myslovsky approached me, and behind him our neighbor. We laughed at our collective insomnia. Then Boris Aleksandrovich asked a question typical of him—like a Shakespearean monologue, and more assertive than questioning.

"I'm not asking in what way the mountains are seductive," he said. "Passion is inexplainable, but understandable. Betting at the races, collecting, traveling, mountaineering—passion stands behind everything. If I don't know yours, I know my own. There is no difference in that the feeling is one and the same... But something else is not clear to me—why is this passion considered noble, why does society encourage it? Why does society permit risking one's life without necessity? You are young and undervalue life, but I value it in and of itself—toward old age it becomes clear: life is life, even if it is unsaturated, unfilled, and so forth. It is valuable for itself. Live yourself and give life to another—there you have happiness, the biggest and the fullest. I appraised life for itself. For four years I did not crawl out from under the bullets and missiles, and I saw people deprived of life. But that was necessary... for the sake of life! Who needs mountaineering, besides the small group of stray people who have had the wool pulled over their eyes by the passion? You think I am a rationalist? Well, no... more of a poet—after all, I'm a mathematician. Society needs emotion and reason to be combined in an individual. But society itself must be rational! So I ask: Why has society legitimized your passion?"

"Everything is clear," Edik interrupted him. "In short, what do we contribute to society? Ah! The utilitarian argument! I once had to deal with that question, and when I told friends about it they laughed in a friendly way—'Here,' they said, 'is what a mountaineer has come to.' You live in Sokolniki, don't you? Well, good. Right there, in the park, I practiced—I climbed in the trees and chopped off boughs, branches, and crowns of pines so they would not fall and cause injury to the strolling pensioners. Who else could do this? There you have an example, small, but close to your heart. Here is another.

"Somehow I clambered onto the Peak of Communism and suddenly, on the plateau, at around six thousand meters, I stumbled upon a strange little hut. Mad scientists lived in it—one Mashkov and a companion. They would come in the door, throw down their ice axes, and grab their scalpels! It was not enough that they themselves climbed to such a height. What is more amazing, they took animals in cages with them—rabbits, rats, mice—and apparatus for testing acclimatization—beakers, test tubes, and whatnot—and a great deal of all sorts of food. I don't know whether the mad scientists ate anything themselves, but those creatures of God (which were not only in pairs) were busy all day nibbling. Perhaps, you think, all that gear was dragged there by train-station porters?

"Or, take geologists. Good people. But they do not go near the place where climbers go. If a geologist would get up to our height he would find ores, minerals, precious stones, and crystals in abundance.

"Not a single structure is managed in the mountains without us. Ask Volodya—he's our boss—how many climbers there are at the Nurek Government Power Station. He will tell you: a lot, but all the same, there are not enough."

Myslovsky was acting as though he had caught a little boy who had splashed him from a puddle, and, having grabbed him by the ear, was teaching him manners. I was filled with laughter.

"And there's more!" continued Myslovsky. "The border

patrol says that to close mountaineering is the same as to throw open the borders—spies will learn mountaineering and will float through the mountains. I had to teach the border patrol our art. By the way, the landing of parachutists in the mountains is a matter not at all compromising, even if unsuccessful experiences have sometimes happened. Fellows landed on the Big Pamir Firn Plateau as though onto an airport field—with special glider parachutes, of course. It's clear that to jump onto a summit or a ridge is suicide. But in the upper reaches of any ravine you can always find a snow plateau—and not too small at that—where a parachute can land without any danger. And it may even be necessary as, say, for rescue work. Imagine that a spaceship landed in the mountains. The cosmonauts need help immediately. You cannot get along without our brothers—the mountaineer-parachutists. Have you heard of torrents?"

"Torrents?" began Boris Aleksandrovich. "It's . . . "

"It's when a high-altitude lake breaks the wall of the saucer in which it's located and rushes downward. Along the way, the water drags everything with it—rocks, trees; it tears off whole layers of soil and comes down in the form of a porridgelike mass. In this way, terrible mudflows move toward cities, but they run into the barriers placed there ahead of time by people and are stopped. It's mountaineers who help the scientists predict the times of possible torrents. It's with the help of mountaineers that barriers are set."

"I'm convinced!" Our neighbor put his hands up. "Really, the simple truth is, if there are mountains on earth, then someone must be able to get around in them. I didn't think—I'm too far from your business."

"By the way, have you heard that during the war, climbers put a cover over the Admiralteyskaya Needle in Leningrad?"

"You defend mountaineering like you would a favorite woman. That's also convincing. It's late, or I would start . . . "

"And one more thing... How should I say it in a shorter way? In short, I think that mountaineering is an injection of courage for the whole nation..."

Boris Aleksandrovich finished his cigarette and went off to go to sleep. I lowered the window. The warm, southern wind burst noisily into the car. Myslovsky laughed.

"It smells of the mountains," he said. "Tomorrow we will stroll around Osh. We'll go to the market... we'll buy a watermelon. Do you remember 1968? What a melon we bought! The two of us could barely carry it."

"I remember. The melon with the drug. You became stupid from it and climbed the walls like Father Fyodor in *The Twelve Chairs*—two times he found himself on summits and didn't know how he had gotten there."

An old joke!" Edik snapped. "You were making similar jokes back in 1968, and you still are now in 1971. You make idle talk. Already three years... You want to judge the winners, but they are not judged, as we all know."

"You yourself know that's not what we're talking about," I replied. "They say that in the war there was an accident. A person jumped out of a burning airplane without a parachute. On the way down he spread out his jacket and planed on it as on wings. He came down in a forest on the crown of a tree—he was injured, but remained alive. Thus, perhaps it would be worthwhile to introduce such a sport—jacket-planing?"

o

Myslovsky and I have a long-standing argument. No matter what we start with, we always end up at the topic of the argument. It began in the Pamirs back in 1968.

I was now going to the Pamirs to climb the Peak of Communism for the third time. My second attempt was the 1968 climb, which followed a route of the sixth degree of difficulty. It was an interesting and complicated climb, and it went without a hitch. At that time, at the foot of this moun-

The Moral Aspect of the Theory of Probability (1971)   135

tain, our expedition had stood at the fork of three roads, so to speak. One of them, as in the traditional fairy tale, led straight toward death.

That "road" was an almost vertical multi-kilometer wall that combined all possible technical difficulties! One comes across such walls in the Alps and Caucasus, but they are half as long and without the ferocious, exhausting altitude. However, this by itself was no reason for crossing the route off as a climbing objective. Indeed, it would be considered a climbing problem, the solution of which one should strive for. We're talking about something else.

We had arrived there around noon. The sun was roasting. Not a cloud was in the sky. The air was hot and still. But there was no silence. Rocks were flying down, as from an ancient fortress during a siege, in a continuous barrage.

Around four o'clock there was a large rock avalanche, but toward evening it became quiet. After seven, when the sun had gone down and things had frozen up higher, the rockfall almost stopped. Only every now and then a cobblestone would crash down from somewhere. It was quiet all night and morning. Then, at eleven, it started all over again and lasted until seven. That is how it always is there.

The wall, however, is promising and tempting—beyond it are titles, diplomas, and medals.

"I can't understand how they could make such a route legal," Gennady Karlov said to me.

"I myself am surprised."

Myslovsky came up: "I'm thinking of going up along the wall. What do you think?"

"I have two children," Karlov answered.

"And what about you, Volodya?"

"I don't go into the mountains in search of death. The opposite—so that my life is happier."

"As you wish. There will be willing ones."

There were willing ones. A group of climbers, with Myslovsky in charge, set off on the wall. They chose the only possible tactic: They left at dawn, worked a section, hung perlon, and by eleven, when the sun was warming the rocky areas held together by cold, they had descended and got out from under the wall. The main thing was not to be under the wall. Even being on the wall was less dangerous, as most of the rocks would fly over you.

We followed a different route, and not an easy one. Like the wall, it was rated at the sixth degree of difficulty, but there was a difference.

One does not have to speak of safety when discussing mountaineering. Although our craft is maturing, it is caught between technical difficulty on one side and safety on the other. The farther the distance between them, the greater the prestige. Determining technical difficulty is clear; let's talk about safety.

Let's assume that it is within our power to make all climbs no more dangerous than a tram ride. What, then, would remain of mountaineering? And what does the expression "safe mountaineering" mean? In my opinion it is meaningless. One might as well remove the oxygen from a molecule of water and call the remainder water. But how to combine this view with the mountaineer's main problem: the search for optimal safety?

There is no contradiction here. We cannot "remove" avalanches, stop rockfalls, hold back slides, patch crevasses, "turn off" gravity, saturate the atmosphere with air, or level out atmospheric pressure. All these are objective obstacles that pose objective dangers. They are the basis of mountain climbing. If such hazards did not exist, one would not speak of "mountain climbers" but of "mountain walkers." ... The art of a mountaineer is to *avoid* dangers, to fight them, to neutralize them with the help of skill and primitive, non-automated equipment—ice axe, hammer, pitons, and ropes. This last point is essential because mountaineering implies more than simply attaining a summit in the easiest way possible; there are also philosophical, ethical, and psychological considerations. Precisely so. For what else is philosophy but the striving of a person to know himself. To understand the meaning of genuine values? After all, up above, it becomes more obvious what is good and what is bad; what is actually important and what is really nonsense that only seems important; and what is a part and what a whole.

Moreover, it seems to me that mountaineering is a test, and the mountains a testing ground or, if you like, a laboratory for selecting the optimal forms of human interaction for clarifying the most viable standards of ethics and morals, for checking how strength gets along with weakness and the strong with the weak, for learning what is genuine strength and what is genuine weakness, and for finding out who indeed is strong and who only wears a mask. (Of course, life itself conducts such an experiment on level ground. And on all of humanity. But the mountains answer all these questions more exactly and more convincingly.) There, with the help of a small group of people, one can demonstrate to skeptics that humaneness is the most useful and advantageous principle of coexistence. Finally, nothing is as convincing as mountaineering that for humans spiritual bread is no less essential than physical bread....

The fathers of mountaineering, in their searches for the greatest safety, are afraid lest at some point they lead it to the ideal, lest they provide the climber with a hundred percent guarantee of safety and absence of harm, and in this way castrate the sport. They know that no matter now much success they have in this area, the risk of climbing will remain. Even if they were to halve the remainder, the mountaineer would still experience a sharp thrill. However, even a war is possible only when there exists some minimum chance of survival.

Mountaineering will become immoral if it sanctions even those climbs where the chances of survival or death are equal. No, fifty-fifty is an immoral proportion. The probability of survival should be overwhelmingly greater. Yes, the theory of probability has its moral aspect. It must serve as an apparatus for establishing moral standards.

People can ask, "How can one determine the exact standard of safety of this or that route?" One cannot do so exactly; one can approximate it. That's what experience is for. And such assessment is much less debatable than it seems. The rating of routes according to degrees is generally agreed upon without any particular controversy or complications.

Thus the expedition from Chelyabinsk, after long observation of this wall, concluded in an official report, "Survival is one chance in a thousand." This was said figuratively, of course, and was in addition greatly exaggerated. But looking at this route, I saw that the chances of remaining alive on it were too small.

In the beginning of this book I said that if a superhuman fearlessness exists, it is not known to us climbers. The mountaineer knows fear—he is human. But another feeling lives inside of him. To paraphrase a proverb: the eyes fear but the soul is drawn. An incomprehensible, inexplicable force draws and hypnotizes him like a blow to a rabbit. An irrepressible fervor, similar to the passion of a gambler, pushes him to overcome danger. Risk gives a fullness to the sensation of life. I have noticed that there are different types of fear. Not only in the quantitative sense—more or less—but also in quality. There is fear with a tinge of panic and there is another, "sweet," fear.

I was drawn to this wall. I understood Edik Myslovsky and his friends well. But if I had surrendered to the temptation, I would have behaved contrary to principles that I advocate often, everywhere, and perhaps even importunately. Internal convictions aside, but simply because of my position in the mountaineering community, I am obliged to temper this trend in climbing, to help encourage a proper sense of perspective in mountaineering. In addition, I think that every climber should be concerned about the ethical purity of

The Moral Aspect of the Theory of Probability (1971) 139

mountaineering, should guard its honor, so to speak. That honor will often be sullied if the sad glory of climbers sentenced to death is dragged behind us.

I do not want, nor am I able under any circumstances, to reproach Myslovsky—a prominent, talented climber, one of the leaders of present-day mountaineering—for athletic immorality. His views and mine on this score, as well as the views of most of our friends, do not diverge. He went along this route, because he firmly believed in the tactics he had selected. He thought that using such tactics would endow the wall with a new quality, making it peaceful and innocent. And to prove the validity of this belief, he used the most weighty, indisputable form of argument: With a group of friends he completed a brilliant, intelligent, beautiful, and accident-free climb to the summit of the Peak of Communism along this wall.

Nevertheless, my attitude, based on principle, toward this route has not changed. As before, I think that achievement is connected more with the talent and luck of the climbers than with the approachability of the route.

It can happen, for example, that the nighttime temperature might be only barely low enough to hold the fragments of rock in place. Then, less time is needed to warm the rocks. Then the rockfall begins not at 11:00 A.M. but, say, at ten or earlier. Even assuming that one can foresee all this and leave the wall with a reserve of time, there is still no way to prevent all possible delays: someone gets sick or is injured, the visibility decreases drastically. There is a lot that can happen in the mountains! The probability of such a trivial delay, especially on a difficult route, is so great that with time—and not much of it—it becomes almost unavoidable. And that probability increases the longer the overall duration of the ascent and the more times a party is on the wall. If conquering the wall lasts, say, not ten but fifteen days, then the chance of a delay is increased one and a half times. By leaving the wall with enough time to spare, and thereby shortening each day's actual work period, climbers increase the overall duration of the climb. As the duration increases, so does the possibility of being late. And being late is synonymous with death.

Therefore, I argue that only prominent mastery, the skill of the group, and good fortune brought Myslovsky's party success. The smallest shortage of one thing or another could have led to tragedy.

I think it would have been good at the time to have a "round-table" discussion about the correctness of such routes. And I pointed this out to Myslovsky.

Overall, that expedition was a great success. I can say this without stretching the point in the least. Myslovsky's group, as I have said, reached the summit via a problematic wall. I led a group of four—Igor Roshchin, Gennady Karlov, Nikolai Alhutov, and myself—up the Peak of Communism by one of the most difficult routes. In the whole history of mountaineering it had been done only once, ten years before by Kiril Kuzmin's team. Besides that, we completed a first ascent of Peak Pravda in this same area (5b degree of difficulty).

o

We were carried away with the argument and did not hear Elya come out of the compartment. She sneaked up unnoticed, gave me a flick of her fingers on the back of my head, and said, "Well, midnighters, have you climbed the walls again? Watch your strength..."

"Why?" said Edik. "I'm not planning to go to the Peak of Communism, and as for Shatayev, he's now going to do no more than walking along a hometown street. It's true, something special is in store for him—a family climb. One needs a little strength for such matters..."

"In order to carry me in his arms?"

"There was no such thing even in my thoughts..."

"You men are thick-skulled, conservative, and self-assured," Elvira started, not hearing Myslovsky. "Nothing convinces you. You live according to principle: If the facts are against you, that means the facts are incorrect. And your tactic toward a woman is to resort to complimenting her eyes..."

"Why?" begged Edik with a laugh. "I didn't have anything of the kind in mind..."

"Shatayev told me," she continued, " 'Don't count on a special position in the group.' 'The group,' he says, 'will not work for you.' As though I was counting on it. He knows I'll die, but I won't give away my rucksack, I won't agree to carry a kilogram less."

"You're very mistrustful, you women," I answered. "It all seems to you that the individual in you is undervalued. We value a person, but at the same time we take into account the real strengths."

"Okay. Everything will be fine, next year we'll get together a women's group and go do a seven-thousander. We'll show that we can get along without you."

She proved the truth of this. Not completely, but at least as far as she was concerned. Without waiting for 1972, she proved it in less than a month.

10. In Pursuit of the "Snow Leopard"
(1971)

I arrived at the base camp and immediately fell ill with tonsillitis. I do not remember where or how I let my throat catch cold, but I know that lack of caution was the main reason. The tonsillitis was acute—I lay for several days with a high temperature. It served as a most sobering "punch," and I set off onto the slopes of the Peak of Communism much weakened.

I was in charge of the climb but was walking at the rear. It was awkward, but there was nothing to be done. At first, I proceeded as usual, stamping one hundred steps, but I realized doing so was not within my strength. The fellows noticed and suggested that I bring up the rear. They were right: For me to lead was not good for the group. Overestimating the strengths of one member of the team can ruin a climb.

It would have been even better to have left two or three days later. That would have been enough time for me to recover. The forecast had permitted it. But something else had not permitted it: One of the participants was in a hurry to get to the USSR climbing championship in the Caucasus. I will call him Pyotr Petrenko. He was a strong mountaineer, one of the strongest of our athletes. He needed only one peak—the Peak of Communism—to earn the title "Snow Leopard," which is given to those who conquer all four of the seven-thousand-meter peaks in the country: Peak Korzhenevskaya, Peak Lenin, Peak Pobeda, and the Peak of Communism. The present climb would bring him the respected title.

I was glad that a strong group had been gathered: Most of the participants were leading masters of mountaineering.

Little time remained until the championship. Therefore, for Petrenko's sake, quite a tight schedule had been established for the ascent and descent. In four days we were supposed to go to the summit by the following route: along the Great Pamirs Firn Plateau to the Great Barrier (6,900 meters), then along the west slope to the summit.

○

Why is hell presented as dark, seething, and boiling? I saw it. It was perfectly white, perfectly quiet, perfectly hardened. Above it there was a perfectly blue sky with a perfectly motionless, hanging, evil, scorching sun. All this perfection was hell. It was not at all a cave—it was a cirque, a concave cup.

Hell—it was an oppressive homogeneity. It deceived with its perfection. Unnoticed, but quickly, it wore one out, brought one to a near catatonic fatigue, with its motionlessness, noiselessness, and monochromaticity. There was nothing to hold the eyes, nothing to listen to, nothing to feel besides the uniformly burning sun. There was nothing besides the perfect white stretched over the whole world, the silence, the coolness. In order to experience hell's tortures, one has to be there no less than an hour.

We descended to the bottom of the cirque—it had a diameter of about one hundred meters—and in twenty minutes we had lost our strength. We needed to leave sooner, but our legs would not obey—I just wanted to lie down and close my eyes. All the same, reason is stronger than the body, like a twig across which a saw is dragged. The mind was still strong enough to subjugate the body to its will. Sluggishly, moving our legs with effort, we went into the hollow . . .

Now I was walking and glad of it. It was good that there was a wind, that there was thunder, that the cliffs were unattractively gray, that in addition to the gentle slopes there were lethal abysses, a steep incline, crevasses, avalanches and rockfall, that all these crossed our path and fell to the left and to the right.

We walked quickly—we had to hurry. The schedule required that we reach the firn plateau by evening and there, having overcome the difficult way along the deep snow, to approach the caves. Otherwise Petrenko would be late for the championship.

But it was strange. For some reason, he was hurrying less than everyone else. The whole time he trudged along at the rear, stepping in prepared, well-trampled tracks. Somehow, this back-line position did not fit his tall, strong, wide-shouldered figure. In front, Igor Roshchin was breaking trail almost without relief. Valya Grakovich relieved him as much as he was able, which was only occasionally.

The team moved upwards in a long, drawn-out chain. The topography changed—rises, hollows, gendarmes, couloirs. Our elevation increased steadily, and, as before, Roshchin was in front. Behind him were Valentin Grakovich from Minsk, Elvira Shatayeva, myself, Vasily Koutun and Aleksandr Fomin from Kiev, and Georgy Korepanov from Leningrad. Petrenko was the final link in the chain.

When I stopped the group and said that Roshchin had to be relieved, everyone looked at Petrenko. But he remained impeccably polite, making way for others, and was silent, probably afraid of interrupting others' initiative. Elvira, also not saying a word, went in front. Now the column displayed a "mirror" arrangement by size: Elya, the smallest, in front, and Petrenko, the largest, in back.

She had prepared less than a hundred steps when Valya Grakovich finally satisfied himself that this was an amazing arrangement for a mountaineering party, one that would not be corrected by moral pressure. He went out to relieve her.

On Peak Parachyutistov, at an elevation of 5,800 meters, where the plateau begins, Petrenko and Koutun stopped, took a tent out of a bag, and began to prepare for the night. According to the plan, we were to sleep in the caves located about halfway across this mountain plain. We still had several kilometers to go. Petrenko's behavior was completely incomprehensible: If he hung back, there was no reason for us to hurry.

I suddenly thought that we were being unjust toward him. What are muscle and weight at such a place? Altitude could weaken even Ilya Muromets.* Petrenko simply felt he would not make it to the caves, although he did not show it and was holding up well.

I spoke with Elvira. She smiled ironically and without answering me, said loudly for everyone to hear, "In my opinion, one should at least try to complete one's plan. After all, we're not novices—we knew our strengths when we made our plan. We can always manage to put the tents up."

"I'll go in front again," said Roshchin.

"And I can work a little," Grakovich said in support.

Everyone looked at me, expecting a decision. I said that there was still enough time and ability, that I myself was intending to go farther, but that it was not obligatory for everyone—those who wanted could set up tents.

Petrenko, Koutun, and Fomin stayed, and five continued and reached the caves after dark.

The next day began at six o'clock. We woke with difficulty. Our sleep had been deep but too short to resurrect our strengths after the previous day's trip. We crawled sluggishly out of the caves, but the weather was cheering: sunny and

---

*A character in Russian folklore who is exceptionally strong.

cold but with absolutely no wind. The colors, sharp and blinding, literally gave sound to the silence.

We cooked breakfast, finished the meal at eight, and by nine, as we had agreed with the three who had stayed at Peak Parachyutistov, were ready to continue the climb.

Sitting on our rucksacks by the entrance to a cave, we talked "about life" and looked at the point where the line of our tracks intersected the line of the curve of the plateau. I was relating something about an international mountaineering contest that they wanted to hold on the Peak of Communism in 1972. The idea, by the way, was Anufrikov's.

Igor Roshchin laughed. "You'll have to tramp along this path a fourth time."

"It's still unknown."

"Everything is known. Who then if not you?" Valentin said. "You're like a guide here now. Three times . . . "

"Numbers are not for me! In Italy I heard a story. On the summit of the Matterhorn two guides met—an Italian and a Swiss. Both had led clients. The Italian invited the whole company there on the summit to celebrate his milestone— three hundred ascents of the Matterhorn. The Swiss did not object, but asked shyly if they couldn't also celebrate his own record. On that day he had climbed to the summit for the six hundredth time . . . "

"The Matterhorn is not the Peak of Communism. Barely half the height," said Korepanov. "And after all, it's their work—the greater the number of climbs, the greater their bank account. Not for a love of the mountains, but for money. Exploits for hard cash . . . "

"That's unfair!" interrupted Elvira. Up to now she had been listening absent-mindedly, looking into the distance where the plateau changed into a slope. "Volodya has told me a lot about them. I understand that they are genuine climbers. And the men are real knights. True, it's their bread. But honor is dear to them just as it is to our fellows. They don't change it for money or for a title. Every day they take risks and are willing to sacrifice themselves for a comrade, not hiding behind others' backs but sharing their last crumb. They are true to the laws of the rope no less than we. In the mountains, they forget that below, a fee awaits them. There are bad people among them. But I'm sure that, as here, such people are the minority."

Elya's opinion coincided with mine when I was in the Alps. But little did I know then, sitting on my rucksack by the caves, that within a year I would be back in Switzerland and would again see for myself that these were true words. Little did I know that two years later, on a joint climb with professional Swiss guides in the Caucasus, I would fall into a situation where I would see with my own eyes the courage and faithfulness of these people, where I would understand that a mountaineer is a mountaineer, in whatever conditions he lives, that his ethics are independent of geography, and that mountaineering is an international brotherhood....

At eleven the group finally gathered together and set off. The plateau is technically simple. There are no crevasses there; climbing is not required. But on the other hand, the snow falls loosely and so deeply that at times you "walk" tens of meters on all fours, making a trench.

We hurried, stomping out our steps faster than usual, moving our legs, but... a miracle, a circus trick! As if in a dream, we floundered, remaining in the same place. Who said that motion is relative? That is only below. If a tram increases its speed, then the street dashes by faster. Our "street," although passing at a gallop, did not budge.

Our "street" stretches twelve kilometers—from Peak Parachyutistov to Peak Kirov. At first, with a slight, barely noticeable descent, it loses about two hundred meters toward the center, and then, at the same angle, it rises to its initial mark of 5,800. At its widest it is about two kilometers. Our "street" has only one row of "structures"; they are on the right: Peak Leningrad, Peak Evgeny Abalakov, and Peak Kuybiyshev. On the left it drops off abruptly—the avalanches we observed from the meadow come from here.

Our "street"—the Great Pamirs Firn Plateau—is unique: it

is the highest of the large plateaus. The air on it is so rarefied that it does not block cosmic radiation. Knowing this, scientists intend to build a scientific hut-laboratory here in the near future with special equipment for detecting aliens from outer space.

We walked across a thin, compact crust of ice that covered the snow and that itself was lightly covered with snow—the walking was easy now. We looked in vain at the summits, but there was no way to reach them. Constantly, every ten steps, we looked behind us, our eyes searching for confirmation, wanting proof, that we were in fact moving. Behind us a long track stretched, changing into an unbroken line and vanishing into the distance. But nothing changed in front— Peak Kirov was just as far. That cursed summit could drive you crazy—it had not moved a meter.

Suddenly we discovered that the mountains all had "passed," leaving some kind of strange, dialectic gallop, unknown below. Unexpectedly, we were at the very end of the plateau—before us was Peak Kirov itself....

In three days we ascended to an altitude of 6,900 meters reaching the Great Barrier, where we spent the night. On the fourth, leaving the last bivouac, we set off onto the summit slopes. Igor Roshchin was in front as before. The large figure of Pyotr Petrenko loomed as usual in the rear. Igor was relieved—not for long, but several times—by Korepanov, Grakovich, and Koutun. However, on the entire route he remained the principal leader.

More and more the altitude nailed us to the slope, and every movement was procured by will. The leader rested every five steps. At the 7,200-meter mark Roshchin stopped, leaned on his ice axe, and hung there powerlessly. I came up and saw that he could lead the group no longer. The sun had been in the west for a long time, and unfortunately it was moving in the direction of the horizon much faster than we were. And we still had three hundred meters to go.

I realized that we would not make it to the summit and

said so to the group sitting on the slope. That was obvious to all, even without my words. But it was also clear that if the summit was not for today, then this time it would not be at all.

"We'll rest a half hour and then begin the descent," I said to the group. Then everyone heard Petrenko's voice.

"I'll go first," he said. "I'll go to the very summit. The climb needs to continue. We must have the summit. There remains only a trifle—three hundred meters!"

It's true, some three hundred meters remained to the title of Snow Leopard! . . .

He went out in front and moved like Jesus on water. Since we had forced every step to that point, his movement seemed like a miracle. He walked easily, quickly, leaving comfortable tracks. He was like a frisky boy playing outside after languishing in the house, or like a poet possessed with inspiration. Cheerful, resilient, happy—it seemed that for him there was no steepness, no altitude, no sodden path.

He walked to the cliffs themselves, not once looking around, not worrying about what or how things were behind his back. We fell behind, even though following in prepared tracks. We lagged behind him by one to one and a half hours. We observed him crossing the cliffs and stopping when the sharp snow-covered ridge rose before him. To traverse it alone would be insanity, and as must be clear to the reader by now, this athlete did not lack a sound mind.

He stopped and, having remembered us, waved his ice axe in a friendy manner. Then he climbed over the cliff ledge and was hidden from view. An hour later we reached the ridge. But Petrenko was not there. It was not surprising: I did not think for a minute that he would decide to go along it alone. We should search for him in the vicinity of the cliffs. The question of why we should look for him at all occurred to me only briefly before it was swallowed by my growing anxiety.

We ransacked the cliffs, searching in every corner, peering

into niches, examining hollows. Finally, in spite of logic, we studied the slopes as much as the glare permitted, but there were no tracks anywhere. We called to him—we shouted, cupping our palms like megaphones. But in response we heard only the mountain echo.

I was preparing to radio the camp about the supposed misfortune when suddenly Elvira's voice rang out.

"Volodya, wait!" she shouted. "I found him."

She had discovered him in a snow niche, "warm," comfortable, and well sheltered from the wind by a drift. He was half lying, half leaning, with his back to the wall, his hands slightly spread, his head resting on his chest and . . . snoring loudly.

We did not say a word to him—there was not the place for such discussion. Instead, we divided into twos and set off onto the ridge. At eight o'clock that evening the setting sun sprinkled the summit for the last time and illuminated the rejoicing climbers.

The descent took place in the dark. At 7,300 meters Valya Grakovich finally wore out. Altitude sickness had already gotten hold of him on the ascent. Although we were losing elevation, it was not enough to save him from this illness. In addition, there was the utter exhaustion—our climbing workday had lasted sixteen hours. Grakovich sat down, fell into the snow, and refused to move farther. I lifted him with force and made him walk.

It seemed that the group disagreed with my actions. I felt it, but acted as though I did not understand. I knew that I could not avoid having to explain my position, but I did not have the confidence to insist on having my own way. I wanted to postpone the discussion as long as possible, in order to descend at least a hundred meters more.

At 7,200 meters Elya took me aside. The others approached us. They sat down in the snow, but I announced: "We'll talk standing up."

"People are tired," Elvira said. "They can't walk any more."

"I am too. What then?"

"What you feel is not the issue. We're talking not about you but about the group. If you were alone, you could deal with yourself as you pleased. You could even go to the summit again if you had the desire to decorate it with your grave. But you are in charge of people, and you are taking advantage of the fact that, for them, discipline is a sacred matter."

"Clear. What do you want?"

"We need to bivouac, Volodya!" Korepanov said, panting. His voice sounded hoarse and strained. The words flew out like the groans of a trumpet in unskilled hands.

"Where? On what? Under what?"

"Let it be cold. But there is no more strength to go on. Another fifty steps and we'll collapse."

"Cold? At 7,200 meters?! I ask those who remain alive to remember my words: Pneumonia will finish off half of us by morning. If I were alone, I would not take a step more. I would act as I wanted, not as I should. But tomorrow I must lead all of you to the meadow. All! I'm categorically against a bivouac. We will go down, even if at a leopard's crawl. And we will spend the night in the tents—three hundred meters remain."

I turned and moved downward. I walked without looking around and heard steps behind me. They were walking! If some were walking, then all were walking. Blessed is the mountaineer's discipline!

At two in the morning we were in the tents at 6,900. We lit the stoves, heated some tea, and went to sleep in warmth.

11. Thoughts about the Living
(1971)

They say that bad things remain in your memory longer than good things, a thought originated by people who live monotonous, uniform lives. They *do* remember more of the bad because their "good" is so uniform, so mundane, and so dull that they can't remember it. Any unpleasantry, even the smallest, is a deviation from the flat, eventless line of their lives, and is therefore remembered. But if the line is interrupted, if it oscillates in peaks and valleys, if happiness is difficult, obtained in battle and adversity, if a majority of valleys crowd at the base of a single, large peak, then the peak itself looks better and its memory is retained more firmly.

Not two days had passed since the descent, when I began to feel oppressed by being in the meadow. I was in the mountains, but I was not on the mountains. For a mountaineer, the meadow is not the mountains.

In the evening, drinking tea in the company of Roshchin, Fomin, and Grakovich, I said to them, "Perhaps we should climb Korzhenevskaya?"

"What a golden thought!" said Igor. "Who's against it?" Everybody was "for."

Early the next morning we four set off for Peak Eugenia Korzhenevskaya (7,105 meters).

We had overcome the highest point and were on our way down when back in the meadow, events were transpiring that seemed innocuous but would turn out to be very important.

○

It had already been a year since Master of Sports Blyuminar Golubkov, a mountaineering instructor and Moscow engineer, was found below the summit of the Peak of Communism at an elevation of 7,350 meters, at his last bivouac. The altitude, the time, and the weather did not harm him—he was dead.

Golubkov's team, led by the Master of Sports Boris Efimov, had completed a high-altitude traverse from Peak Leningrad to the Peak of Communism. The fellows experienced every hardship that such a difficult and extended traverse could unleash: mountain sickness, bad weather, extreme fatigue, sleeplessness, undernourishment...

Blyum, as his friends called him for short, was already feeling bad on Leningrad Peak. But who feels good at such altitudes? How do you recognize the permissible standard of health? And where do you pack the apparatus with which to measure it?

There remained less than one hundred and fifty meters to complete the traverse when Efimov's team met another party on a small, gently sloping section. Among the climbers was a doctor, Vladimir Mashkov. Golubkov's condition worried Efimov, so he asked the doctor to examine him.

After the examination, Mashkov took the leader aside and said: "Down, immediately!"

Both turned around to confer with Blyum, who sat on his rucksack, his head hanging low.

"Blyum!" Boris turned to him. But hearing no answer, he repeated, "Blyum? What, did you fall asleep?"

Blyum had not fallen asleep. He had died.

They did not have the strength to take the body down themselves—they had no strength. They barely had enough to get themselves down—they crawled to the meadow by will alone.

Never in the history of mountaineering had a body been brought down from such an altitude.... Abroad, climbers leave the bodies of perished friends in the mountains for eternity. Their reason is that to risk additional deaths in an attempt to carry a body from one grave to another makes no sense. Unfortunately, such has happened more than once.

In my country we risk our lives in order to return the body of a friend to the bosom of the inhabited earth because our hearts order us to do so. We follow lethal paths to retrieve the remains according to the call of the soul. The transportation of a body is complicated and dangerous, and foreign climbers, when the subject comes up, accuse us of superstition. And their argument is understandable; their logic is clear. It is difficult to say anything against it. Only not everything is measured by logic....

Perhaps the question is beyond logic. For the mountaineer is happier and more at ease if he knows that in the event of an accident, his remains will not become part of the forsaken wilderness. Perhaps he rests easier knowing that people will record the special significance of his life by risking their own to bring his body down from the mountain so that it will lie closer to them. And if that is so, then bringing it down is, after all, in the long-term interest of mountaineering.... and by reminding the living about the sanctity of human life, perhaps this practice has far-reaching implications for the future of mankind as a whole.

All the same, every time I learn that people have perished while transporting a body I renounce my own views on this. Then I think, one should sacrifice life only in one case—to save a life.

I cannot hide this contradiction because it is impossible to be silent on the subject in a book about mountaineering. And I am not sufficiently competent to dispute either of these positions.

o

And there, as we were attempting Peak Korzhenevskaya, seven climbers under Vadim Kochnev's leadership were working with a transportation sled to bring Blyuminar Golubkov's body down. At first there had been twelve of them. The twelfth, Georgy Korepanov, had fallen sick with pneumonia after one of the acclimatization trips. When he recovered, Kochnev had let him go instead with us to the Peak of Communism. When we had set off for this summit, we had taken with us part of the transportation load to drop off at Golubkov's grave. Korepanov had been a participant in that sad traverse and knew where Blyuminar lay.

Eleven rescuers had remained. While we were descending the Peak of Communism they were going up. We had met them on the plateau by the caves (5,600 meters); they had to get to the 7,350 mark and from there drag the loaded sled.

But things turned out worse than they had expected. The weather turned bad, and from the plateau to their goal they were accompanied by an icy wind against which no kind of climbers' insulation could hold out. By the time they reached the body, four of the eleven turned out to be sick. Kochnev quickly sent them down.

The difficulty of transporting the body now lay on the shoulders of seven. They pulled the sled toward the summit of the Verblyud gendarme, at 5,200 meters. They had covered about two-thirds of the way, but there they were finally worn out. Vadim Kochnev radioed the camp asking for help.

The radio message arrived as we—Grakovich, Roshchin, Fomin, and myself—were descending from Peak Korzhenevskaya. Elya received it. She sat and maintained contact with the rescue party since she could not do anything else. Her toes had been frozen on our climb, and the doctors had given her an anesthetic. Now she could walk only by stepping on her heels.

The meadow is never empty, and there were plenty of people. But apart from Petrenko, Korepanov, and Koutun there were no masters of mountaineering, people capable of setting off to help Kochnev's party. Elvira turned to the masters.

Koutun immediately said he was sick. It was also bad to count on Korepanov—the inflammation in his lungs had knocked him out of his usual form for the entire season. He had survived our climb in worse shape than many of the others, and there in the meadow he was still weak.

Having spread out his clothes underneath himself, Petrenko was resting against his prepared rucksack, taking in the mountain sun. He was waiting for the helicopter. He had already been waiting several days to get to Osh and from there to fly to the Caucasus. They had kept postponing the helicopter, but now they had announced that it was on its way.

In any event, Petrenko was no longer in a hurry; he was not tormented with impatience, nor was he nervous. He was late for the championships anyway. Now he could be only an observer, not a participant, in the Caucasus.

Elvira herself, in spite of her injured foot, immediately lay hands on her boots, although she understood that nothing much would come of it. But she could not remain by herself off to the side, summoning others to noble deeds, could she?

"What will we do?" she turned to Petrenko.

"I can do nothing. I have to go to the championships. Besides, Shatayev released us. Act as though the helicopter arrived on time and I have already left."

The helicopter soon landed. The inhabitants of the meadow—where, as a rule, everyone always knows about everything—watched tensely, holding their breaths, as Petrenko headed for the machine. He walked slowly, barely waddling, his head lowered lazily, as people of his stature usually walk.

Everyone who wished it so saw in his slow gait the appearance of spiritual hesitation, of indecision. Everyone waited; his movement was on the point of fading completely. He will stop, they thought, shift from foot to foot, and turn back. But instead he walked up to the helicopter and climbed lightly into the cabin...

The motor roared. The propeller started. But the revolutions thinned out, and Petrenko appeared again in the door of the fuselage. He jumped down and quickly, almost at a run, dashed toward the group of women surrounding Elvira.

They looked at him as closely as one looks at a man who has jumped over the railing after being acquitted by a judge. Elya later related that he said he had completely forgotten about those in need of help. It seemed to her that the one who was genuinely suffering was Petrenko. She wanted to save him. And how much lighter her heart became when they saw this happy self-rescue!

The "saved one" approached the women and said, "Girls, where is my Turkish bowl? Has anyone seen it?"

Elvira was the first to come to her senses. To shame him, she wanted to be subtly attentive, even obsequious. She strained her memory and recalled that they had been drinking tea together in the tent of some people from Dushanbe.

"Girls, indeed, where is his favorite Turkish bowl?" she endeavored. "Look for it, please. Let the man fly away with a calm heart."

They found the bowl. Petrenko headed toward the helicopter and in a minute disappeared into the belly of the machine.

And Elya went to her tent, buried her head in her pillow, and began to cry. Her hysterics lasted until late at night. They could not calm her in any way or with anything. The camp doctor gave her several strong tablets, but they were of no more use than candy drops.

It seems to me that belief in a person is a matter of instinct, a force that impels people to unity and mutual action. All societies, in one way or another, work out ideals that are shared by everyone, ideals toward which the society strives and in which it believes. If ideals exist, societies exist. If ideals do not exist, then there can only be disconnected individuals unsuited for life. In order to live, a person must possess the ability to erect ideals and believe in them. To repeat, I think that this ability exists in us as an instinct, with all the force thereof. When instinct is thwarted, the reaction may be stormy.

Elvira was one of those people in whom this instinct is particularly well developed. Later she told me she had felt betrayed. "Maybe everyone is like Petrenko," she thought. "They only pretend, act self-righteously, and play the knight. Perhaps this is all only a theater, a traveling circus. Perhaps my Volodya too ... and I, like an idiot, believe ... It turns out that I am simply an unintelligent, naive person. And in their hearts they all laugh at me. Perhaps Petrenko is the most genuine of them all ... "

I have talked about Petrenko in order to emphasize the high moral standards of our mountaineering. They say that the exception proves the rule. I can add that the stronger an exception deviates from the rule, the more trustworthy the rule is.

At ten in the evening we arrived at the meadow. While I was undressing, taking my boots off, and washing, they told me about the situation of Kochnev's people. In half an hour Grakovich and Roshchin came to me in my tent.

"Well then, shall we put on our boots?" Valentin turned to me.

"For the time being, slippers ... Let's go to the radio."

Making contact with Kochnev, I asked whether they could wait until morning. And I heard the answer: "Definitely."

Early in the morning—it was not yet five—we left the camp in a threesome. At nine, having covered thirteen hundred vertical meters by the shortest route, we were standing on the upper point of the Verblyud gendarme. We had taken with us six hundred meters of three-millimeter steel cable weighing fifteen kilograms, a pulley, a brake of Grakovich's own design and construction, and various other items for transportation.

Valentin is a person rich in both intellect and athletic ability. His talents would more than fill five lives: He has a Ph.D. in geography and was champion in military-mountaineering sports, an excellent mountaineer, rock climber, and rescuer. And, as happens in people with inquisitive minds, he had a flair for inventing things. It is good that this latter passion has an outlet—mountaineering equipment. Knowing about Kochnev's expedition, he flew out to the Pamirs, bringing with him the fruits of several of his design efforts—just in case anyone would need them. We did indeed. They saved strength, shortened time, and to some extent lowered the degree of danger.

People lowered the body along the cliff ridge, which was shifting so much it seemed to be moving. They drew out three fixed-cable paths, losing three times as much time on them as they had planned. The heavy sled, sagging, slid along the cable and, from a distance, resembled a fairy-tale boat floating miraculously in the air.

Darkness approached quickly. It became obvious that we would not finish the descent that day. But we continued to work as long as we could see.

A steep snow and ice slope stretched downward from the 4,500-meter level. I fastened myself to the cable and set off alone with the body. Rocks were screaming by, breaking away from the ridge. It was already impossible to see them— it was dark. They rumbled close-by: above, below, to the left, to the right. Somewhere above me, Grakovich and Roshchin were letting out the cable, but they too were not visible. It was terrible, perhaps as never before. Even now I am not myself when I recall that sad connection with Blyum's body.

We descended four hundred vertical meters with him. But

at the 4,100-meter mark, the dense mountain night overtook us. In the morning Valentin Grakovich relieved me. He set off with the sled down a narrow, deep chute. All the rocks channel there, everything falling from above. But there simply was no other route. It was good that it was morning, when only infrequent, incidental stones fell from the frozen, hardened slopes. But there were enough stones so that our lives were hanging by a thread. These last two hundred meters were no less for Grakovich than the preceding four hundred had been for me.

Two hours after entering the couloir Blyuminar Golubkov's body reached the base camp in the Suloev Meadow. Later, by air, it arrived in Moscow.

12. The Pamirs
(1974)

Safe mountains do not exist. Mountains are birds of prey. Sometimes they sleep, full and gratified, for many years. Then it seems to people that they are tame. Then everyone, even the most experienced, careful, and circumspect, is lulled by their tranquility. The precept that there are no safe mountains is gradually erased from memory.

We were walking along a tranquil mountain, along sloping, serene, peaceful slopes, more like level winter fields than the flanks of a seven-thousander. Only the light was violent. It seemed that if that fierce illumination were to increase even slightly, there would be an explosion. Everything else had crystallized—the sun, the air, the sky, the panorama... all seemed extensions of the thick, rounded snowdrifts. Heavenly abundance. Here a child could go sledding! Where was the danger here?

The danger is obvious on peaks like Khan Tengri, and on Peak Pobeda, the northernmost seven-thousand-meter summit in the world. There hurricane winds invade and subzero temperatures are cruel. There, on Khan Tengri and Pobeda one needs to think through every contingency, to consider unexpected situations, to foresee the unforeseeable. But here, on Peak Lenin, everything is known, everything is understandable, everything is calm....

We related to this mountain as to a tame dog whose fangs hold no danger for its master. For forty-five years we had been relating to it in this way, as if the pressure here were inoffensive and the rarity of air were not suffocating. We would ascend to seven kilometers into the sky without doubting the outcome, as assured as if we had been going to Seventh Heaven in Ostankino.*...

Forty-five years—from the day of the first assault—Peak Lenin had been as meek as a lamb. Then it bared its fangs...

o

I was climbing Peak Lenin for the second time in two weeks. They did not let me go, they tried to dissuade me, they forbade me. I explained, tried to convince them, and assured them. Finally, I broke loose. Why? In order to see her one last time? Of course. But this is only part of the truth. I couldn't tell them about the miracle I was hoping for, about the microscopic, infinitesimal hope that even I believed not in my mind, but in my heart!

On August 8, the day after the terrible events, when things had settled down and the weather cleared, the Japanese had left their bivouac at 6,500 and for the second time set off in search of the women's group. They found them on the summit slope. The bodies lay stretched out one after another for two hundred meters, from 7,000 downwards, like a dotted line on a piece of paper. There were seven of them. That is what our foreign colleagues had informed the camp.

Seven, but where was the eighth?

And *who* was the eighth?

Unfounded hope, not a single real chance. Had she descended to a forsaken but inhabited place in the Pamirs, now, three days after the catastrophe, we would have known about it. A minute hope hung in the air, supported only by

---

*A restaurant on a radio tower in the suburbs of Moscow.

the force of my desire. I tried to give it support, thinking up fantastic variants, but not one of them added up. I know — it was stupid. Yet still I hoped... I had to search for the eighth...

People from Chelyabin were with me. There were four of them, friends of the Chelyabin mountaineer Valery Perehodyuk. His wife, Galina Perehodyuk, was one of those who lay at the top... Yet one more mountaineering couple separated by the mountains. He was straining with us... For him too "the eighth" was a shaky hope.

We were going too slowly. Or did it only seem so?.... The pain accumulating inside me was stronger than any drug. I tried to increase the pace, but instead I only spoiled the regularity of the climbing step. Besides, it was not possible to move faster. There was twice as much snow as usual. Breaking trail was difficult, as at no other time. One had to make the tracks carefully; otherwise one disappeared into the depths, in over one's head, so to speak.

A strange summer. The old-timers did not remember such a snowy summer. Two weeks before, on July 25, I and Master of Sports Dainyus Makauskas, my personal and climbing friend, had approached Peak Lenin from the southwestern Pamirs. (There we made several trips with mountaineers from East Germany.) Along the road we saw sheep tied up in the snow that covered the alpine meadows. The shepherds were chasing the large flocks down into the Alaiskaya Valley, thinking that there they would save the animals from hunger. But the valley also was the whitest of whites. During the night of July 25, an unprecedented storm had arrived and turned the mountains white to the very foothills. The international mountaineering encampment in the Pamirs was located in a meadow under Peak Lenin, at 3,700 meters.* A meadow is a meadow because it is green.

---

*This Soviet-sponsored "International Alpiniade" was a gathering of prominent climbers from several Western countries (including the United Japan, and Eastern Europe. — The Editor.

We found this meadow covered with a layer of snow about thirty centimeters deep. Later that same season, it snowed twice more.

At exactly that time, on July 25, when the snowfall covered the area around Peak Lenin, the American foursome led by Gary Ullin had completed the climb of the Peak of the Nineteenth Party Congress. Suddenly they felt a strong tremor. Now, earthquakes are frequent in the Pamirs. But as a rule, the seismic waves, moving away from the separate epicenters in the region of Afghanistan-Tashkent, arrive in a weakened state. This time the blow was no less than four points, enough (and then some) to set in motion a mass of snow that was already poised to fall.

A huge avalanche covered the Americans, but the experienced mountaineers were able to free themselves. They ascended upward along the avalanche track and set up their tent there, obviously figuring that the most reliable shelter from projectiles would be a snow crater. Any possibility, however small, with time becomes certainty. It was possible what would then occur had not happened for a thousand years, and would not for another thousand, but it happened then. A second avalanche hit the climbers and dragged them downward. Three managed to break free, but the fourth, Gary Ullin, one of the strongest American mountaineers, perished.*

---

*Shatayev's version of these incidents differs from that of Bob Craig, as told in *Storm and Sorrow* (The Mountaineers, 1977). According to Craig, he led the American team, which included Gary Ullin. At the time of the fatal avalanche on July 25, the team had not reached the summit of the Peak of the Nineteenth Party Congress ("Peak Nineteen"); they were poised to try the summit climb that very morning. The earthquake had occurred on July 23; it was preceded that day by a huge avalanche close enough to the American team to send snow and ice particles drifting over their tents, but did not cover them. The second avalanche occurred on July 25. It covered the tent of Bob Craig and Gary Ullin, causing the tent to collapse; the climbers were not dragged from their campsite by the avalanche. The other two team members, John Roskelley and John Marts, were able to dig out Craig, but when they uncovered Ullin, they found that he was dead.—The Editor

At the distress signal, a helicopter took off and dropped food to the Americans, as well as wands to mark the location of the body. A rescue team of Soviet, American, and French climbers quickly set off from the base camp to meet them. Ullin was the first victim...

o

The ill-fated snowfall of the night of July 24/25 found the women's group in a cave at 5,200 meters. They were on the second acclimatization trip, which was to take them up to 6,000 meters. According to a scientific and practical schedule, an ascent to this level would make them sufficiently accustomed to the altitude and give them a reserve of acclimatization for a subsequent climb a kilometer higher yet.

Thus it was planned, but it turned out differently. The dangerous snow conditions and Gary Ullin's accident forced the camp boss to order everyone off the slopes. Such was the situation Dainyus and I found when we arrived at the Pamir international camp.

We did not linger at the meadow even an hour. They asked us to ascend to 4,500 and inform the leader of the American team, [Peter] Schoening, of the death of Gary Ullin. (His bivouac was located behind a bend, and the Vitalki radio works only in direct line.) Along the way we met the returning women. We gave them a letter and said they should expect a visit from us later that day. They exchanged glances secretly, examined each one of us with precision from top to bottom, and answered nothing.

In camp we started to look for the tents of the women's group. But we were told, "Shatayeva's team is living on that side of the stream, behind the fortress wall, and entrance there is by special pass."

We set across—more exactly, we stepped across—the stream and began to look for the fortress wall. We found it: a thickness and height of one "brick." In truth, in the absence of bricks the wall consisted of a white dotted line made with little stones laid out in a circle.

The guard—she was the cook on duty—was Ira Lyubimtseva, and she was armed with a steaming ladle, evidently just withdrawn from some concoction. Hearing our steps, she jumped out of the kitchen tent and immediately gave the signal. A garrison poured out of the Pamir tent. Dainyus, having accidentally stepped across the "wall," was immediately grabbed and thrown outside the boundary of the fortress.

Elvira, maintaining the prestige of leader, remained in her residence observing the ritual. They reported to her. She came out ceremoniously and, examining the "intruders," asked, "Who are they? What do they want?"

"They claim to be guests," answered Ella Muhamedova.

"Guests?"

She turned around and, giving the signal, led everyone away except Valya Fateyeva, who remained on watch.

They put us off for about fifteen minutes. From the tents could be heard female hubbub, interrupted with frequent bursts of laughter. Then Lyuda Manzharova appeared, holding in her hands clean sheets of paper and a pen. Without taking note of us she gave them to Fateyeva and said, "Let them write an application. Each one separately. They can make just one copy—we're not bureaucrats."

We wrote: "We request you to receive us since we very much want to eat."

Nina Vasilyeva finally came out and announced, "The council has examined your application and considers the reason valid. The council has resolved to issue a special pass."

Having announced us as guests, they showed us emphasized politeness and concentrated attention for some time, trying not to fall out of their roles. This amused everyone, and everyone wanted to continue the performance a little longer. But sometimes they would forget and let out provocative bursts of flirtatious laughs toward us, the men. Finally Tanya Bardasheva said, "It's no good, girls!" And turning to us, she added, "Don't be taken in by them. They skulk around here looking for someone to ridicule."

The Pamirs (1974)

Dainyus answered: "A hunter once told me that bears always love it when bees sting them. But the hunter, as always, probably lied."

A pretended commotion arose. Feigning indignation, they taunted us: "Just think, we're bees and they're bears!"

They communicated with half words and mere glances, and orchestrated the banter as if reading the parts of a play.

They had come together ony two weeks ago—on July 10 in Osh. Many of them had seen one another for the first time then. Elvira had known some of them from previous climbs but others only through correspondence, begun in January 1974.

After that evening we spent another two days in the female fortress, having received permission to set up a tent (of course, they enclosed us with little white stones).

They were disciplined and lived like a well-schooled ship's crew. They were precise in giving orders, punctual in carrying them out, and aware of their obligations and individual roles. Not once did we hear words of argument or contention, nor did we see sulky lips, dissatisfied expressions, or condemning looks. Their behavior put to shame the Eastern proverb that "Two women are a bazaar."

Strolling with me by the tents, Elvira nodded toward a small, trampled grass plot and said, "That is our assembly hall."

"What, you dance there?"

"That too."

"You're great; you've created a unit."

"Irony again?"

"No. For real."

"Have I really lived to hear your praise? A miracle!"

"It's true, this is a rare group of people gathered together—simply ideal—and you were the one who brought them together. Right?"

"Ideal? We don't think so. Sit in one time on our discussions. You'll understand: Deficiencies are piled high in everyone. Besides myself, of course." She looked at me mischievously, laughter hidden in her eyes.

"I know, you're perfection. It turns out, you also openly criticize one another, and I thought only . . . "

"And you should read the minutes. You men have never dreamed of such openness. We agreed: If you speak, then speak in full—everything that we think about each other. It's disturbing to feel reservations, when it's obvious that a person was not frank, when something remained in her heart. It may be that the 'something' is only a molehill. But, after all, you make a mountain out of a molehill."

"Okay, and how is criticism taken?"

"They all react differently. But there is no offense. The women are intelligent—they all understand the reason for criticism."

"Once again I say: great. Character flaws also need to be made open so that each person knows he is not a secret to others. Then each person becomes himself and doesn't hide behind a mask. Then you see the real person faster. When you know a person it's easier to adapt to him. Once again, I advise you to check the group well for compatibility, and if someone is a problem, count her out. Don't be afraid of being severe. Softness in this case can be fatal for everyone."

"We have already dismissed one. An egoist who talked too much and loved public notice. She belayed not as though you were headed for the summit, but as though straight to heaven. The girls refused to go on a rope with her."

Little by little the camp fell silent. The voices in the women's tents quieted down. All that could be heard was a humorous song accompanied by a guitar from somewhere on the other side of the stream:

> *Oh, how affectionate you are,*
> *My little mountaineer, my climber.*

And soon these night birds fell silent. Still I could not fall asleep, and the catchy refrain kept circling in my head. I knew that Dainyus could not sleep either, and I said to him, "There you have women. To find such order in male groups..."

"True, but I'm thinking about something else. They hit at one point—we women, they say, do not give in to you men in anything. As if in jest, ironically."

"Not 'as if'—precisely in jest. They want us to be stronger, and they love us for being stronger..."

"That's what we always think. And they think so—they think they want this. And all the same, 'as if.' They have a conflict... an eternal conflict."

"A conflict with nature?" I asked.

"Exactly. Latent, trodden into the subconscious, and accumulated generation by generation. Why do these women try so hard? Because it is their fate to express that conflict, to defend their ability! Our skepticism has hung over them for a thousand years."

"It's no great loss for us... it's their own!"

"Precisely. What happens? They have ascended the mountaineering Olympus. They have scrambled up. Torn to pieces, scratched all over, turned into one complete bruise, but they've scrambled up. They were victorious in battle. In which one? In the physical one! They came out on top of 'Olympus' and believed in their fighting qualities. Only look, that skepticism is still above them, as it was a thousand years earlier. They are standing on this 'Olympus' next to us, and they see that we are surveying the panorama from a level one head higher. But in the excitement of victory it seems to them that they can overcome this difference too... if they stand on their tiptoes. And there they stretch. You can't, after all, stand like that for long—"

"I'm afraid it seems so not to them, but to you," I interrupted Dainyus. "After their climb of Peak Korzhenevskaya and Ushba, I decided that the Lord God himself didn't know a thing about women."

"It's possible. I'm not arguing. I'm only telling you how it appears to me. And in addition, it seems to me that in making a fetish out of discipline, they are—how to say it?—subjugating themselves. They know that one of the cornerstones of mountaineering is discipline. They admire the fact that strong, healthy, strong-willed, independent men know how to subjugate themselves in this way. I think they admire it because for themselves this is difficult to do. In my opinion they are most afraid of the reproach that women have gotten together and therefore what kind of discipline can there be? This then is their number-one worry—not to give any grounds for such a reproach . . . to behave so that not one thing can be said against them. Here then is my worry—that they are taking on too much. I'm afraid that they are trying so hard that they are developing not discipline, but obedience —discipline without initiative and without independence. If you investigate the matter, you will find that even in the most independent women independence is a weak spot. Reliance on the protection of men is set in their genes."

Earlier, Dainyus and I would not have disagreed on this point. But events of the last two years had shaken my opinion. If the reader remembers, back in 1971, while on the train to Osh, Elvira half jokingly promised Myslovsky and me a climb of a seven-thousander by a women's group [see Chapter 9]. All during the winter of 1972 she selected the team. The following summer that team of four, under the leadership of Galina Rozhalskaya, and which also included, besides Elvira, her friends Ella (Ilsiar) Muhamedova and Antonina Son, conquered Peak Eugenia Korzhenevskaya (7,105 meters).

That was the first successful women's climb of a seven-thousander in the world, although there had been attempts before.

The next year, Elvira organized and led still another

women's expedition, which completed a traverse of the legendary Ushba.

These facts are indisputable.

However, Dainyus was still right about one thing, although the truth of what he said only served to emphasize, to magnify, their feat. One can only guess to what degree masculine skepticism burdened their work. In one of the articles devoted to the first women's climb of a seven-thousander, Elvira wrote: "The psychological barrier—overcoming it is one of the basic tasks of our pioneering climb.... And the retort of skeptics—that women cannot survive even twenty-four hours without excesses—made us cautious. Perhaps it is sometimes true."

They justly believed that women were being judged by their conduct, that the slightest slip would call forth the exclamation "Women!" And the main thing was that, given the opportunity, this cry was ready to burst forth from their own mouths. They tried to conduct their campaign calmly, without haste, and with masculine endurance and rationality, repressing their female emotion. All of which made them self-conscious.

They were modest in their female self-assertion; they did not assert that theirs would be an athletic "great leap forward"; they did not wish to reduce the world to amazement or to win applause. For these athletes the climb was only the next step in their development, following naturally upon their previous accomplishments. They set off on the climb, though with doubt in their hearts: Was it beyond their limits as women? And was it not also "taboo"? Therefore, they approached the task reasonably, cautiously, fearing above all to overestimate their own strengths. While still in Moscow, Elvira said to me, "I want to conduct the climb under the motto 'The quieter you walk, the farther you get'."

She said the same thing to Volodya Kavunenko, who was trying to convince Elvira to go to Khan Tengri [in the Tien Shan range of central Asia—Ed.].

This northernmost of the earth's tallest summits can be compared to the Himalayan eight-thousand-meter peaks in difficulty, although formally it does not appear on the "list"; it does not even reach seven thousand, being five meters shy. A severe chill flows from the pages of this mountain's history. In base camp, at an elevation of 4,000 meters, snow storms rage in the middle of a hot August summer. People fight their way with difficulty from one tent to another. You can imagine what it is like on top. A large part of the year a mighty layer of clouds hides the summit. It seems as though the clouds are attached to it forever, like an umbrella to its handle. The clouds are as unshakable as the mountain itself. Avalanches arrive with the frequency of subway trains. The weather changes quickly, sharply, and unexpectedly. Not without reason is this region called "the rotten corner."

Kavunenko was trying to convince Elya to go to the Tien Shan because he himself was planning to assault Khan Tengri. He pointed out to her that there was nothing so terrible about the mountain. Sometimes a five-thousand-meter peak that you approach casually will make things so difficult for you that afterwards you won't want to look at mountains for a year. At other times, on a normally inaccessible summit like Peak Pobeda, the sun will break through and hang around the entire route. The cooperation of the two climbing teams, he said, would lighten the task and bring success to both.

Like all of us, he was a little afraid for the women. Knowing that business might take me away from where the women were planning to climb, he had decided that it would be better if they were closer to him. Then he could stand by unnoticed in case of an accident. But Elvira was not drawn away from the theme of "A Women's Climb." *Women's!* She immediately saw through his ploy and announced to Kavunenko:

"You think we are not serious? But it's you, in reality! After all, Volodya, we are not after prizes. Perhaps at times there is sense in deceiving others, but why oneself? Remember: the biggest skeptics in this story are the women themselves. Do you understand? I myself do not fully believe in myself, although I have been on Ushba and Korzhenevskaya. I argue with myself, and I'm going to Peak Lenin in order to prove it to myself once again. And you gentlemen, you see, are inviting me to walk arm in arm to Khan Tengri."

It is not difficult to evade unwanted guardians; though, of course, she did not refuse for this reason. Rather, she understood that for the time Khan Tengri was not yet within their ability.

They did not want publicity, loud newspaper articles, or excessive premature praise. Shortly before leaving for the Pamirs, Elvira wrote to Ilsiar Muhamedova:

Hi Elka!

Let's begin to count down the days until we meet. It's already close. Joy without end. I want to congratulate you once again on "women's day"—the day we established our group.

Is it worth giving vent to one's feelings? In this way everything is clear. Only it's still unbelievable.

I have some business for you. First, don't forget to bring the medical-examination card with you. Second, I don't know whether it's possible or not. The tent in which you lived with Galka in the meadow is good. Would you be able to get such a tent? Of course they'll give us one, but evidently a "Pamir" tent. And third. Store your favorite thing (candy, cigarettes, or anything else) in your own personal dish at the "ladies' table."

Our bosses, V. M. Abalakov and V. N. Shatayev, believe us and believe in us very, very much. I think that we'll not let them down. Good women are getting together.

Elka, I'm very superstitious. For goodness' sake—no interviews to anyone. Let us leave in silence, okay? I wouldn't want any kind of mention, not a line or a word. Although they already know in the Union, so let them know. But nothing new about yourself, about the group, or about the climb. Early publicity has no part in our business.

    Did you understand the hint?   Kisses, Shatayeva

When I awoke the next day, July 28, it was not yet six. The canvas tent was yellow, like stained-glass windows illuminated from behind. I opened the flap and saw a clear sky, a bright sun, and naked mountains. It seemed there was not a single cloud in the whole hemisphere.

I woke up Dainyus and showed him the weather. Having greeted each other with a "Good morning," we began to load our packs without useless conversation. In an hour only little white stones remained in remembrance of our stay.

Before leaving I looked into the tent at Elvira. She was sleeping, so soundly that a damp spot was visible on the pillow opposite her lips. Looking at her, I recalled Evgeny Tur's words, spoken somewhere in a magazine article: "When they tell me that mountaineering makes women coarse and masculine, I always bring up the example of Elvira, her grace, her femininity, and her unusual spiritual generosity."

We left them a note that we had gone "for a walk" to Peak Lenin, and went to the camp to file a claim for the climb. Along the way we met an acquaintance from Leningrad. Learning of our undertaking, he said, "What, have you gone mad? Two in such snow? You won't make it to five thousand—you'll die!"

We will get there. With our acclimatization, an eight-thousander is possible. During the last month we had registered at that height, so to speak. The weather and our athletic condition gave all the grounds for counting on success.

On July 28 we climbed to 4,500. It would have been possible to go farther, but we decided that was enough for the first day. On the other hand, by evening the next day we had left one and a half vertical kilometers behind us, and we set up camp at the 6,000-meter mark.

Tired, but feeling like people on their birthdays and regretting that mountaineering does not have spectators, we went to bed. But before falling asleep, we gave ourselves an ovation, and that was enough for us.

On the morning of July 30 the weather was as good as before and made our climber's fervor burn. Having thought a little, we left the rucksacks and the tent, gulped down a can of juice each, and set off.

By 4:00 P.M., all 1,150 vertical meters to the last centimeter were downhill. Peak Lenin was beneath us. It took ten minutes to replace the summit note, which lay in a cairn by the bust of Vladimir Ilyich. Then ten minutes of happiness—which this time was especially intense. Was it perhaps because the climb had been accompanied throughout by the constant sense of preciseness, competence, and speed?

At 4:20 we began the descent. A bank of dark gray clouds had accompanied us on our approach to the summit. Now, a strong wind spun the falling snow. Visibility was ten to fifteen meters. The small track on the last section was swept away in a quarter of an hour.

The situation was not simply difficult—it was critical. The tents, the rucksacks with food, the stove with fuel, and the equipment remained in the camp at 6,000 meters. We had to descend, but where? There was no choice. There was only one way out: to rely on our mountaineer's "scent." Otherwise it would be a cold night out—on the summit and in such weather.

The wind poured from the south, beating our faces with hard, biting snow. Hunched over, almost sticking our knees into our foreheads, pausing every two or three steps to wait out the unbearable gusts of the blizzard, we still moved downward, almost blindly. After an hour, even with our limited visibility, it became clear to us that we were on unfamiliar slopes. It did not matter which way we went, just so long as it was down.

Is it possible that we walked out of this maelstrom, that the weather simply began to calm? Yes. Soon the wind weakened, the sky cleared, and it became warmer. Downward the slope fanned out. Dainyus was the first to notice and joyfully shouted "A broom!" We were lucky because a route well known to the climber is called a "broom"...

That day we descended to the cave at 5,200 meters. There we found everything we needed: food, bags, equipment, and the main thing—a stove with fuel. We spent the night full and warm. The next day we climbed up to 6,000, packed the tent, and returned with full rucksacks.

Approaching the "inhabitable" altitude, we noticed from afar the familiar Pamir tents and understood—the women. The caves were not to their liking, and they had set themselves up on the surface, pitching the tents about twenty meters away. Elya, Nina Vasilyeva, and Valya Fateyeva met us. The rest were already sleeping. All three started to busy themselves with dinner.

We began to relate our adventures. Dainyus mentioned deliberately, as if in passing, that we had climbed from 4,500 to 6,000 in one day. We still wanted applause—and we expected it. Nina, circling her eyes in amazement, said, "One and a half thousand? Two in such snow? Did you hear, girls?"

"Such information is harmful for us," Elvira broke in. "Girls, remember: Don't take it to heart, as they say in Odessa. We are on our own. We will not begin to compete with others: They have their own tasks, we ours. Theirs will never agree with ours—let them try to complete a women's climb!"

"That's not the point," said Dainyus. "It happens that men sometimes walk like women. Volodya and I saw it once. Six men were hiding in a niche, waiting to die. We had to use force, physical force. We slapped three on the cheeks. The rest went by themselves. Now every holiday they send us telegrams with best wishes."

"Yes," sighed Elvira. "We don't have sufficient crude masculine strength. Okay," she concluded. "Let it be so:

Pants are good, a dress is bad. But we will remain in a dress. We will not start trying to imitate men; we will not try to compete. We will create our own style of climbing—a feminine one, since we don't have to and can't walk the way men walk. There's no place to hurry to. Our scheduled closing date is August 9, and by that time we'll have completed the traverse over Razdelnaya."

Their task was a traverse of Peak Lenin. In specific terms that meant ascending by the route across Lipkin's Cliff, crossing the summit, and descending on the other side across the summit of Razdelnaya. Such was the plan. Understandably, our women considered it inviolable, more sacred than we men would have in similar circumstances. We would have looked at it simply: If the traverse succeeded, good; if not, no matter—there was still the summit itself. They considered this alternative impermissible if they were to avoid being stereotyped as "women."

They fed us cutlets with buckwheat porridge, and gave us tea with jam to drink. We ate with appetite. Smiling, Elvira looked openly at my mouth—she liked my appetite. In parkas and with ice axes they were still women. In only about ten minutes what I had eaten was on the snow. Elya began to worry, but my condition was such that I was ready even to go to the summit again.

"Don't worry. Everything is normal. That's the way it is for me on the second day. You know—it happens with altitude."

Then we put on our rucksacks. But before leaving I called Elvira aside and said, "If you see that anyone is at the limit, leave your things. There are tents at 6,500 meters. Storm the summit and return along the ascent route—to hell with them, with the traverse! Do you promise?"

"What are you talking about, Volodya? If someone gets sick, no sort of summit will come to mind. We'll begin the descent immediately. But if we climb to the summit, we'll not begin to give up the traverse. Understand—it's uncomfortable for us. If the base orders—that's a different matter..."

"The base may not know your situation."

"We'll not hide anything. We'll present everything as it is."

Dainyus was already waiting for me about forty steps below. I moved in his direction. But having gone a short way, I turned and shouted, "See you soon in Moscow! Invite all the girls to our place!"

We arrived in camp at 11:00 P.M. We figured the whole trip had lasted eighty hours, with all the wandering and the repeated ascent of eight hundred meters, from 5,200 to 6,000.

Having accepted the congratulations of friends, we went to bed.

Work called me to Moscow. In the morning we went by plane to Dushanbe and flew home the same day.

o

On August 7, 1974, a telegram arrived at the USSR Committee of Physical Culture and Sports from the Pamirs international camp. It told of the death of the Swiss climber Eva Eissenschmidt as a result of extreme weather conditions that had developed in the area of Peak Lenin. That evening the deputy president of the committee, V. I. Koval, and I flew to Osh. We arrived in the night and immediately made radio contact with the camp. On August 8, over the air came the words: "A big accident has happened..."

13. Catastrophe
(1974)

" ... Two participants falling ill when the team was on the summit significantly complicated the position of the group and furthered the tragic outcome.

" ... The basic reason that the group perished was the extremely complex meteorological conditions that arose suddenly, the hurricane winds with snow, the sharp drop in temperature and atmospheric pressure, the lack of visibility...."
—from the conclusions of an official commission

August 13 —our third day. Only three of us remain. Three times three is nine. And there were eight of them. No. At first there were nine. One didn't fit in with the others. They excluded her unanimously... Sokolov's down parka is torn. Where did he tear it? I wonder whether you could fly in a strong wind if you spread your parka out wide? How about a padded jacket? And if you devised a harpoon and shot out a rope with a contraption for catching hold of things? In any bad weather, in zero visibility: Shoot and it catches. Drag yourself up. And another forty meters forward. With such a device they could be saved, perhaps. The stupid sun burns without limits. Who bound my face with gauze? Oh, yes... Davydenko just came up and said that I had a blister on my cheek—sunburn. He tied the bandage for me, but I didn't notice. Then I suddenly remembered; I wanted to tear it off. Then suddenly I remembered again—they were not going to let me go, but I promised that everything would be alright... "Okay." The Americans are strong fellows. To them, everything is "okay." When I asked whether they had marked it well, whether we would be able to find the body later, they said "okay." After, I saw Schoening cry.... And everything will be "okay" for me too. They worry in vain. Why did I take on the leadership? Why? Everything probably... It happened that way. Where did he fall sick? About three hundred meters back... Evidently altitude doesn't agree with him... And I myself sent him down with an escort. It's true, there were five of us—now three. Three? It's true—Davydenko, Sokolov, and myself... Need to go ahead... "Sokolov! Let's change. I'll go first." Damn! What terrible snow! No way to trample it down... and silence... If only somewhere, something would fall with a crash. If only an avalanche would let loose. This cliffy ledge is like a cat. I don't like cats. They're malicious and deceitful. But Elya loved them. She's trusting. That's why she also loved cats. She couldn't be deceived. Is it a shame? That's not the word. She was gentle... Was? Was! "The mountains are smiling"—poets look at them from below... Is it really a smile? It's a cat's grin... It's a silent guffaw... Stop! But where are our shovels? Did we really leave them at the bivouac? What will we use to dig a grave? Damn it!... There it is, under the rucksack flap... and if they had suits with electric heaters? Tiny accumulators? Or nuclear sources? And a seal on the latch: "Open only under extreme circumstances." And oxygen? A canister? Also with a seal? Another ten kilograms on their backs? And how about with pressure? I want to cry out, to howl... to go somewhere behind the bend and yell at the whole Pamirs. To blow up this idiotic silence. How could such a thing happen? After all, there were people around. Korepanov with his group on the far side, Gavrilov's team on this side. After all, Kostya Kletsko was there! Japanese, Americans... Some five hundred to six hundred meters away. It is astounding. But why isn't something else astounding—when there are a dozen doctors at a dying man's bed, and

Catastrophe (1974)

he dies, and nobody can help him? "You can't bite your own elbow"—now it's completely clear what this proverb means... Maybe the most dramatic figures in this tragedy are those who were right there and couldn't help. I wouldn't want to be in their place... So we didn't find traces of their bivouac at six thousand... It still was a good bivouac. Elya reported from there: "We've reached six thousand meters. We're resting. The stove is already hissing. Moods are good." That was at 8:00 P.M., August 1...

Every step brought us closer to the terrible place. Not long until the meeting—some two or three hundred vertical meters. We've had radio contact with base camp several times. And every time I've secretly awaited a miracle; every time before turning on the transmitter, I've dreamed of a voice: "Volodya, she's been found." Although still back at camp, someone said to me, "The Japanese seem to have identified her." "Seem to": dull scissors—they don't cut so much as crumple and make a hole. All the same, I believed. But the faith diminished with each new radio contact, with each meter of elevation. Finally, I said to myself, "Enough of being fooled. She's there, on the slope by the summit." From that second on, belief in miracles vanished as if by the touch of a hand. I prepared myself for the meeting. I was afraid of her, afraid of myself. I was a climber now, a leader. I promised that everything would be in order. Moreover, I wasn't allowed a last meeting. Business. Of everyone in the camp, I alone remembered them well in their mountain clothes. I played on this, using it as a formal reason that, toward the end, proved useful in convincing everyone who had tired of trying to dissuade me, to convince me...

They needed to identify them and compile a description. A description was obligatory. In a year they would take them down and give them to relatives. Who would take them down? I would, I hope. But anything can happen. A record is necessary.

The portable tape recorder, a Sony, under my sweater

pressed against my ribs. I was holding it there so that the batteries would not freeze. It was irritating, but I didn't feel the pain. Who would do the recording?

The fellows were somber. They walked bent over, their hoods pulled down over their eyes, watching underfoot. They were bent not so much from fatigue as from the impending rendezvous. I knew that they foresaw a scene, a terrible scene. Where would I get the strength so that it wouldn't happen? Only one thing was clear: At seven kilometers elevation, nobody should get on anybody else's nerves under any circumstances. Only then did it become clear what kind of moral burden they had taken upon themselves when they agreed to go with me.

The ridge was not far off. Somewhere there, at 1:00 P.M., August 2, Elvira transmitted to base camp: "Only an hour left before we get onto the ridge. Everything is going well. The weather is good, a slight breeze. The route is simple. Everybody's general state is good. Everything so far is so good that we're disappointed in the route."

Little is known about what followed. There is only one source: the radio transmissions reconstructed by me from the words of those who participated.

Later that day, at 5:00 P.M., the women's report to base camp was no less cheerful and optimistic than their 1:00 P.M. communication. The camp wished them a good night, and the transmission ended.

August 3, 8:00 A.M.

Elvira: "... We decided to take a day of rest."

Base (V. M. Abalakov): "Elvira, things are clear to you. It will be as you decide. Don't hurry. A good forecast is in prospect."

Gavrilov's group was on its way to meet the women's team from above after an assault on the summit. The Master of Sports Oleg Borisenok was on the radio, heard the women's announcement, and transmitted to them, "We're coming to you. We'll see each other soon and have a talk."

Catastrophe (1974)

August 3, 5:00 P.M.

Elvira: "I'm correct in having us take a day of rest."

Base: "Don't have doubts. It's clear to you. I trust you. You made a suggestion—I agreed."

Elvira: "Tomorrow we want to reach the base of the summit—to cover a lot of ground on account of our rest. Perhaps we'll make an attempt on the summit."

On the morning of August 4, somewhere at a higher point, Georgy Korepanov's group was moving upwards, climbing from the other side. By evening, having reached the summit, they had begun the descent, and by dark they had managed to drop several hundred meters in the opposite direction, toward the summit of Razdelnaya. Between these three moving dots—Shatayeva's, Gavrilov's, and Korepanov's teams—and base camp, regular transmissions were being maintained—sometimes directly, sometimes by means of an intermediary group. Vitaly Mihailovich Abalakov was conducting the transmissions from below.

August 4, 5:00 P.M.

Elvira to base: "While we were talking with you, the fellows made Peak Lenin" (she meant Korepanov's group). "We congratulate them (knowing that Korepanov was hearing the conversation). We're envious. But perhaps tomorrow we'll be congratulated. Let Korepanov meet us on Razdelnaya, let him make us tea. We wish Zhora a happy birthday. Best wishes. We're bringing you a present. You've already conquered Peak Lenin; now we wish you an eight-thousander."

Korepanov to Elvira: "I await the present. Come quickly. We'll continue to heat tea for you. Come faster. Do you need this mountain? If they weren't driving me, I wouldn't go."

Elvira to Korepanov: "The weather is getting worse. It's snowing. That's good—it covers the tracks. So that there won't be talk that we ascended along a trail."

At the time of this transmission, Gavrilov's group was

resting next to the women's bivouac at an altitude a little higher than six thousand meters. One of the leading participants of the group, the Honored Master of Sports Konstantin Kletsko, asked for the camp.

Kletsko to base: "What kind of instructions will there be?"

Base: "The girls are fine. Elya made a report. Their general state is great. She announced her schedule. I suggested a little something to them. I think you need to start down and tomorrow descend farther."

However, the Gavrilov people had a much better indication of the women's general state, since they had seen them with their own eyes; they had drunk tea together. In fact, the girls felt good.

August 5, 8:00 A.M.

Borisenok to base: "The weather is good. Warm. We are getting together now and will descend with the Scots."

Base: "Good, if they agree, descend."

Shatayeva's group was still sleeping. There was no contact with them.

August 5, 5:00 P.M.

Shatayeva to base: "We reached the summit."

Base: "Congratulations!"

(The reader, obviously, has guessed that the general strategy of movement of the groups had been thought out, and it presupposed some patrol by male teams during the time that the women were on the slopes—for support, just in case. However, no matter how carefully the fact of the support was hidden, there on the slopes it became an open secret. The possibility cannot be ruled out that it was precisely for this reason that the women were dragging out the climb, trying to break loose from the guardianship and selecting the time of greatest distance from the "guardians" for the traverse.)

At first, the Gavrilov-Kletsko group did not hurry to descend, for obvious reasons. But after receiving instructions from base they moved down, and on August 5 at 5:00 P.M. they reached the Japanese cave at 5,700 meters. At that time Oleg Borisenok was included in the transmission from base to Shatayeva. Finding out that they had successfully reached the summit, he said, "Very good. We wish you a successful and quick descent. Zhora can't wait for his present."

Shatayeva to base: "Visibility is poor, twenty to thirty meters. We have doubts about the direction of descent. We decided to set up the tents, which we've already done. We set up the tents tandem and have already settled ourselves. We hope to examine the path of descent in improved weather conditions."

Base: "I agree with such a decision. If there's no visibility, it's better to wait it out and, in the extreme case, to spend the night there on the summit, if that is possible."

Shatayeva: "Conditions are tolerable, although the weather is not fooling around, and there's no visibility. As we were told, the wind is everywhere here. I don't think we'll freeze. I hope that the night won't be very serious. We feel good."

Base: "It's unpleasant and really cold on the summit. One can't rule out the possibility that the wind will not diminish at all later on. It may be even stronger. Try to wake up early, look around, and find the descent path. And if it's possible, descend immediately."

Borisenok: "Good night. Have a successful night."

August 6, 10:00 A.M.

Shatayeva to base: "The weather has not changed in the slightest. There is no visibility. We got up at seven and have been following the weather the whole time—in case any sort of break appeared in the clouds so we could find our position, so we could orient ourselves for the descent. And here it's already ten o'clock, and nothing, no improvement. Visibility is just as low—about twenty meters. What does base recommend, Vitaly Mihailovich?"

Abalakov: "Let's talk at 1:00 P.M. Have something to eat."

August 6, 1:00 P.M.

Shatayeva (an anxious note is heard in her voice): "Nothing has changed during this time. No break. The wind began to get stronger, and rather sharp. Also, there is no visibility, and we don't know in which direction we should move. We are ready to leave at any moment. But the time passes... We are preparing lunch now. We want to eat and be ready, so that we can get everything together in ten or fifteen minutes, no more. Does Zhora have any kind of recommendation? Tell us whether anyone is coming in our direction."

Borisenok was conducting the contact in Gavrilov's group. He intervened in the conversation.

Borisenok to Shatayeva: "We request a small break. We are making contact with Zhora now."

Korepanov's group was behind a bend and did not have direct contact with the summit. Borisenok called Korepanov and transmitted Elvira's question to him.

Korepanov to Borisenok: "The deterioration in the weather is noticeable on the ridge and lower. Individual climbers are heading up today, but in all probability they won't reach the summit. Anyone who leaves his bivouac site will obviously return because of the bad weather."

Several minutes later Borisenok told Shatayeva the content of the conversation with Korepanov.

Shatayeva: "All the same, where should we go if we stand facing the obelisk?"

Kletsko: "Stand facing the obelisk and begin the descent on the left side..."

Kletsko to Korepanov: "How to descend after that?"

Korepanov: "It's very difficult to consult over the radio. In general, there's no clear descent there, such... intermittent fields. One can descend if there are tracks from a previous group. If there aren't tracks and no visibility, then it's better to sit and wait out the bad weather."

Kletsko to Shatayeva: "If there's bad weather and you can't see anything, it's better to stay in place."

Shatayeva: "We'll discuss it now and make a decision."

August 6, 5:00 P.M.

Shatayeva to base: "The weather has not improved in the least. The opposite, it keeps getting worse and worse. We're sick of it here . . . It's so cold! And we would like to leave the summit and go down. We have already lost hope for a break . . . And we simply want to begin . . . in all probability, the descent . . . Because it's very cold on the summit. A very strong wind. It's blowing very hard. Before the descent, Vitaly Mihailovich, we'll listen to you—what do you say to our proposal? But now we really want to call a doctor to the radio. We have a question, we need to consult."

Gavrilov's group was located at 4,200 at this moment.

Borisenok: "We request Tolya Lobusev to come on the air." (He was located at the camp at 5,300 meters on the side of Razdelnaya.)

Lobusev: "What's the matter? What kind of consultation is needed?"

Shatayeva: "One of the participants got sick. For about twenty-four hours now she's been vomiting after eating. We suspect that her liver's bothering her."

There were questions and answers with the goal of establishing a diagnosis.

Lobusev: "I assume that it's the beginning of pneumonia. The group must descend immediately."

Shatayeva: "We have a small set of medicines." (She listed them.)

Lobusev told them what and how much to take, what to take immediately and what to take in two to three hours.

Shatayeva: "We're in such a situation that we don't know

how to distribute the medicine—one more of our group doesn't feel too well..."

Again there were explanations of the symptoms and the doctor's recommendations.

Abalakov to Shatayeva: "I reprimand you for not having informed us earlier about the sick member. Carry out the doctor's instructions immediately—give the injection—and descend immediately along the path of ascent, along Lipkin's route."

Shatayeva: "I understand. Good. Now we'll give the injection, pack the tents, and immediately—in fifteen minutes—begin the descent. Concerning the reprimand, I prefer to discuss it after we descend, not on the summit."

Mountaineers, like the majority of adults, eat three, at most four times a day. Elvira said she had been vomiting after eating. That meant the symptom had appeared no more than three or four times. It's possible that the sick person did not give it much importance and was silent about her condition so as not to arouse worry in her friends. It's natural to think that if the team had known about this earlier, they would have asked the doctor to the radio during the first transmission.

Another thing. The women did not have any reason to hide the member's illness—the summit had been taken, and after a difficult night it is not likely that they were tempted by the traverse. A climber knows that the alternative would be unnatural. After such an experience ambition, together with strength, leaves a person. Only duty and submission to discipline remain. Both, as is known, were highly developed in the women. Only that restrained them from deciding independently to descend along Lipkin's route. People in their position can dream about only one thing: to descend as soon as possible. It's unimportant how, but for them the best way would have been with a wave of a magic wand. This note rings clear in the conversations. It is easier to imagine that the member's illness would have served as grounds for the group's descent by the simplest way.

But it is also easy to understand V. M. Abalakov. The women had been on the summit for more than twenty-four hours, and in the seven-thousand meter region for several days, in conditions of insufficient oxygen and barely tolerable cold, in conditions where the atmospheric pressure is less than two times normal. He was nervous and exploded, so to speak, when confronted with the unexpected announcement. His nerves were strained to begin with. Any other person in the place of this strong-willed and reserved man would have spoken perhaps even more sharply.

There was no radio contact that day. The women began their descent. But from the morning transmission of August 7, the events of the previous day became known. Having questioned Shatayeva, the camp heard:

Shatayeva to base: "Yesterday at 11:00 P.M., during the descent, Irina Lyubimtseva died tragically..."

Yes, disease has its own time there. A lowland hour is similar to a mountain minute: People die faster from a cold at high altitude than they do from profuse bleeding in the lowlands. I am familiar with the situation of a person losing a friend on a trip. Everything toward which one has strived loses its value and becomes false and evil. They were women broken by misfortune, exhausted by altitude, stiff with cold, yet they found in themselves the strength to resist. On a narrow ridge blown by an icy wind—to the left a precipice, to the right a steep slope—they set up two tents. Only one fit on the widest spot, so they spaced the second one lower.

On August 7 at 2:00 A.M., a hurricane descended on the summit—a hurricane in the broadest sense of the word. How to explain what this means?... A wind that in the lowlands tears off roofs, smashes walls, rips wires, contorts trees, and carries away masts is even more savage at high elevation. There it is fresh, not frayed by obstacles, and a person who happens to be in it is, like a midge drawn into a vacuum cleaner, completely helpless and uncomprehending. The hurricane ripped the tents to shreds, carried away their things—including mittens and stoves—and scattered them over the slope. They did manage to save some things, including—most important—the radio transmitter.

They transmitted the news during the ten A.M. contact. Reception was so poor at the camp that Borisenok had to pass on the message. Within fifteen minutes of receiving the transmission a detachment of Soviet climbers started up from base camp, despite the poor weather. French, English, and Austrian climbers set off independently, on their own initiative, in a hurry to help.

The Japanese left their bivouac site at 6,500 and moved in the direction of the ridge. Two fruitless hours, with the risk of life, of searching in the hazy, raging cyclone. They did everything they could ... alas! Nor could the Americans do anything.

The next contact was around 2:00 P.M.

Shatayeva to base: "Two of us have died—Vasilyeva and Fateyeva... Our things were carried away... There are three sleeping bags for five people... We're freezing, very much, we're very cold. Four have badly frostbitten hands..."

Hearing this information, Gavrilov requested them to make contact with the camp in thirty minutes and to repeat it directly to base. Around 2:30 the group repeated the information for base camp.

Base: "Move down. Don't lose heart. If you can't walk, then keep moving, be in motion all the time. We request that you make contact every hour, if it's possible."

Around 3:30 P.M.

Shatayeva: "We're very cold... We can't dig a cave... There's nothing to dig with. We can't move... Our rucksacks were carried away by the wind..."

5:00 P.M.

Base to Kletsko: "The Japanese didn't find anything on the

ridge. They were frostbitten because of the strong wind. None of the searches have produced results."

7:00 P.M.

Base to Kletsko: "The tragedy is ending up above. In all probability they will not last long. Tomorrow, at the morning contact at eight o'clock, we'll announce what you should do. Probably go up ... "

8:00 P.M.

From above came one more announcement of the group's hopeless situation.

Base to group: "Make a pit, make yourselves warm. Help is coming tomorrow. Last until morning."

9:12 P.M.

Galina Perehodyuk conducted the transmission this time. One could hear them coming on the air, but nothing more—silence. Then crying. It is difficult to understand the words—"request" or "forgive"? Finally ...

Perehodyuk to base: "There are two of us left ... There's no more strength ... In fifteen to twenty minutes we won't be among the living ... "

Two more times the pressing of the radio button was heard—attempts to come on the air ...

August 8, 8:00 A.M.

Base to Kletsko: "Shatayev knows everything. He's coming."

Still one more small, but steep, rise. From above, the slope curves and sticks out in a sharply planed, transverse snowy ridge. Perhaps there, behind the bend. It's already time. I go out on the gently sloping section. In front, about forty steps, a cross-shaped object growing into the snow is visible ... A little higher, another one ...

I want to move from my place, but my legs . . . I grasp my ice axe sticking out of the snow and stare with fear, afraid to find out . . . You can't tell from here—you have to go closer . . . But I know that it's here . . .

Sokolov and Davydenko are behind. They are looking in confusion, and both lower their eyes when our glances meet. They do not know how to behave . . . To overtake me, to approach themselves, or to leave this possibility to me? I need to go . . .

And—I knew it—it's Elvira. She is lying with her face up, her head to the north, hands stretched out without gloves . . .

The fellows tactfully leave the two of us alone and descend behind the bend. Thank you, to them—I need to spend some time alone with her . . .

Someone must dictate what we have found on the tape. The tape recorder is under my clothes—it's not easy to get it . . . and is it necessary? The microphone cord is short. If one of them does it, I have to stand connected and listen to a foreign, businesslike voice . . . to stand and wait . . . It's better myself.

Pressing the start button, I raise the microphone to my lips and say, "Elvira Shatayeva . . . With her feet to the south. Her head in her hood. Blue anorak, down. Black pants, double vibram, crampons on her feet. No glasses. Four meters away, elastic from glasses . . . In her pockets: a carabiner and various female items—a nail file, tweezers, a pencil, a round mirror, broken, cracked. . . .

"Ten meters higher. It seems to be Galya Perehodyuk—it's difficult to recognize her . . . yes, it's her—I recognize her by the cap that Elvira knit for her. Gray down parka. A green belt on her chest. Two carabiners on it—one of them a Papa Karlo. Felt boots on her feet with canvas covers on top. On her hands, red wool socks. The sock has slipped from her right hand, and her ring is visible . . ."

We found all eight. The eighth—Nina Vasilyeva—lay in the tent, which was torn to the crest, under Valya Fateyeva's body. The Japanese had not noticed her. They had studied the situation visually, without touching anything, which they thought might go against national custom, ethics, or ritual.

We dug two graves. In one of them we buried Nina Vasilyeva, Valenina Fateyeva, and Irina Lyubimtseva. In the second, Galina Perehodyuk, Tatiana Bardysheva, Lyudmila Manzharova, Elvira Shatayeva, and Ilsiar Muhamedova. The shovel handles and flags stick up out of the snow above the graves. In a cairn with a piece of yellow material, we placed a tin can with a note that the members of Elvira Shatayeva's women's group are temporarily buried here. In the note is a list of the names with an indication of each one's location.

○

A year has passed. During this time, friends, acquaintances, and unknown climbers have visited me, written letters and called, both at Skaterny Street and at home. They have expressed their sympathy and made the same request—to be included in the expedition that would be sent to Peak Lenin to bring down the bodies.

Strangers named their climbing ratings and listed their merits, at times forgetting modesty and exaggerating, just in order to get on the approved list. Sometimes I told them, "Bear in mind that there will be no summit," but soon realized that I was offending them with this remark.

I will not begin to hide my sin. Hearing this request from strangers, I would ask myself, "What do they want, what kind of gain are they looking for?" I did not find any "gain," but I did find a mistake in my own reasoning. It turned out that my data was incorrect for the problem: they were not strangers, but my own kind. They were mountaineers. It was very important to them to acknowledge this fraternal closeness, to reaffirm it. After all, they knew something else, that solidarity among mountaineers makes everyone stronger. This is valuable knowledge, more of the heart than of the head, but without which a climber's life would be empty. This is knowledge that unifies and that needs our continual confirmation. They requested to be included on the list because they were always searching for an occasion to strengthen this fraternal tie. And perhaps herein lies their gain: to walk in risk and deprivation, but in return to receive a firm, unshakable belief in the fraternity of mountaineers. Moreover, they cannot *not* go because they are beckoned by their own brave hearts.

Competition developed. The number established for the expedition was twenty-five. Applications, oral and written, were around a hundred. How to refuse without giving offense? Not having freed myself completely from the delusion that many would drop out on their own, I kept assuming that their applications were made on impulse. But those turned out to be the minority. All this time, the rest were inquiring about the fate of their applications. I ended up having to resort to a variety of excuses to explain why each was being turned down.

On June 20, 1975, an expedition consisting of twenty-five mountaineers left for the Pamirs. It included the strongest climbers of the country, many of whom the reader has become acquainted with in these pages. There were the International Masters of Sports Vladimir Kavunenko and Gennady Karlov, Masters of Sports Dainyus Makauskus and Valentin Grakovich . . .

Oleg Abalakov had to drop out. Of course, he was numbered among the first candidates, but he was unlucky. In a ridiculous accident, he broke several ribs during a soccer game. Unfortunately, he had not recovered sufficiently by the time the expedition set off.

I was designated leader of the expedition.

Work went strictly according to schedule, without disruptions and without accidents. Everything went smoothly, as on level ground.

An entire settlement of relatives grew up at base camp. After two weeks of difficult work, the bodies of their loved ones were delivered to the meadow. Three were taken home. We buried the remainder there, among them Elvira, erecting a shared monument and individual tombstones for them.

Catastrophe (1974)

The meadow will help preserve their memory forever. As long as the Pamirs stand, mountaineers will always be there...

We are mountaineers. We are testers. In the air, pilots test the reliability of plane construction. In the mountains, we test the construction of a person, his power, his physical and psychological limits.

And testers, it sometimes happens, perish.

Then why does the number of mountaineers grow so quickly? I answer: We have life to envy—even though it may be torn away prematurely. We live many lives. We span the whole history of humanity. In our ascent we return to the basics, to the very beginning of human society, to the same difficult fate that awaited mankind from the first.